MIRIAM DAUGHTER OF FINNISH IMMIGRANTS

DIANE DETTMANN
MIRIAM KAURALA DLONIAK

Outskirts Press, Inc
Denver, Co'

"All these years later, I can still see him swinging the scythe through the field, watching the wind-rows form as he rhythmically swished the shiny, wicked-looking blade from right to left."

Dedicated to:
The Kaurala Family and future generations.

ACKNOWLEDGEMENTS

Thanks to my niece, Diane, who encouraged me to write these pages so succeeding generations of the Kaurala family would know a little of what it was like when we were growing up. I also wish to thank Mary Jones, my niece and Diane's sister, for contributing the wonderful sketch work. Finally, many thanks to other family members, nieces, and nephews who expressed a desire to know more about their roots.

INTRODUCTION

There are countless memories stored in the many chambers of my mind and my heart. Some are painful even yet, while others bring back feelings of joy and warmth. Being part of a large family such as ours, we learned at an early age to think of others. Each of us knew the meaning of sharing; and whether it was wearing an older sister's hand-me-down clothes or helping a younger sibling with homework, we were a family undivided.

We learned to turn our backs on those who teased us and called us *Kaura Pussi*, even though it hurt us deeply. We proved that by being good students we earned the respect not only of other students, but of the teachers, and above all, our parents. When Mother went to night school to prepare herself for citizenship, we were only too happy to help her with her lessons. And when she came home from her evening classes and showed us her grades, we were as proud of her as she must have been of us when we brought home good grades.

Being a part of a large family had its drawbacks as well. From the time I was aware of my existence, at the age of three, I felt unwanted, left out, and over-looked. My two older sisters seemed to get all the attention. When visitors came, I often hid so they could not see me. Most of the time, the conversation at home revolved around Martha; how pretty and intelligent she was, and most of all how much she resembled Father. My other sister, Esther, was so quiet and well-behaved, and she looked like Mother. Then someone would point to me and say, "Now who does *she* resemble?" The comments made me wish I had the power to disappear permanently.

I felt like a non-entity.

This went on until one day I received a compliment that was to sustain me for years afterward. A somewhat older friend of Mother's picked me up, hugged me, and said, "Now, here's a healthy-looking girl." It was the first time I remembered hearing anything positive about myself. Consequently, I took pride in "looking healthy." To be sure, I was a bit on the chubby side when I was a pre-schooler. I was not fat by any means, but in those days, many older people equated chubby with healthy. From then on, I concentrated on looking healthy. It did not matter to me whether I resembled Mother, Dad or the man-in-the-moon. All that mattered was I looked *healthy*. I did not care if my hair, bleached almost white by the hot summer sun, was a sharp contrast to my sunburned fair skin. I did not care that my dark eyebrows gave my face a strange look—as long as I looked *healthy*, nothing else mattered.

As the years went by, I learned to come to terms with myself. I came to realize that Mother and Dad were not being disparaging in their remarks. I finally accepted the fact that I was not Martha, I was not Esther, I was me. Though this acceptance was painful at times, I resolved to be the best that I possibly could, and decided to make the best out of what life had dealt me. I developed a sense of humor that has seen me through some rough times. I learned long ago that beauty is only skin-deep, and that hasty judgments of character based on physical appearance miss the true beauty. True beauty is in the heart.

Some of my memories of those early years are painful. Times were different back then. Wielding a birch bough to the backside of a child to correct undesirable behavior was an accepted method of discipline. The use of physical punishment was frequently found in homes and in the school setting, and at the time was not considered abusive.

I can well-remember the county school supervisors coming to our school with a black rubber hose which was used as a "persuader" for the big, unruly boys. Many of the boys, in spite of being in their early to mid-teens, were often twice the size of the young ladies who were expected to teach them. There were times when the teacher broke down and cried; I remember one of the boys, upon seeing the teacher cry, walking past her desk, patting her on the head, and saying, "Poor teacher."

At home, Mother did the best she could to deal with our misbehaviors, despite the fact that sometimes she had to resort to physical punishment. Often she had no other choice. She could not send us up to our room because we had no room of our own. She could not take away privileges or allowances, because we had neither. At the time, "to spare the rod and spoil the child" was the guiding philosophy not only in our home, but in most other homes as well.

As the oldest surviving member of my immediate family, I have tried to portray my childhood as accurately as I can, to give the younger generation an idea of what it was like to grow up during the years of poverty in the late 1920s and the Great Depression. We had very few luxuries, but we had dreams of better days, and a hope that sustained us through times of hardship. As a family, we worked together to make a home in the wilderness. We played together when there was time for play, and we survived together, to succeed in spite of everything. We learned to love one another, and we grew up with a fierce loyalty to our Finnish heritage and a pride in our family tree.

— Miriam Kaurala Dloniak

Diane's Thoughts

Over the past several years, as I have listened to my aunt Miriam tell her story, I have felt and realized many things about myself, my family, and the time before today. The experience has brought me a new appreciation for the resiliency and depth of character in the members of my family. In the wilderness of northern Minnesota in the early 1900s, my grandparents, Finnish immigrants with limited English skills made a commitment to survive in spite of the bitter cold winters, the poverty, and the hard times of the Great Depression. As Finnish immigrants they had *Sisu*, and for that I am very grateful. If Miriam had not shared her memories and words with me, I would never have had this understanding and appreciation of my family's roots.

Though the process of gathering and publishing Miriam's story has taken longer than either one of us ever expected, the experience has been well worth it. Miriam and I have had many phone conversations between Pleasantville, Pennsylvania and Afton, Minnesota. We have shared laughter, tears, and some frustrations, yet the process has brought us closer together.

— Diane M. Hohl

Original homestead in rural Babbitt. (L to R) Martha,
Miriam, Ora, Mother (Hilja Kaurala), Paul and Esther

Wedding picture, 1917, Ely, Minn., Hilja Lukkairla Kaurala (Mother), Paul Paavo Kaurala (Dad)

THE NEW COUNTRY

"On the ship coming back to America, she met a young man,
Paul Kaurala, who was to become her husband
a few years later."

MOTHER

Mother, Hilja Lukkarila Kaurala, was born on October 8,
1888, near Simo, Finland, which is located a short distance from the
border of Sweden. She was one of eight children, three boys and
five girls. Her father was a harbor master who worked long hours
helping to bring the boats safely into the port. In his spare time, he
worked as a tailor—this is probably where Mother inherited her
magic with a needle and thread.

When Mother was twenty-one years of age, she came to
America to look for the fabled streets of gold she had been told were
here for the asking. After three years of doing housework for the
wealthy members of society, she returned to Finland, but there she
found life dull and unpromising. So, in 1913, she returned to
America. On the ship coming back to America, she met a young
man, Paul Kaurala, who was to become her husband a few years
later. This was a ship-board romance that lasted until Mother's
death in September, 1965.

Before her marriage, Mother worked as a domestic in Hibbing
and in Eveleth. She often told us stories about the families for whom
she worked. As we grew up, she held high hopes that we too would
get employment as domestics. I have often marveled at how she
was able to cope in a strange land where she was unable to speak

the language. She had a limited education and no special training, but she was still able to succeed quite well. Yet, she was no worse off than the thousands of others who came to America at that time. Immigrants had to accept America at face value. They often had to make it on their own with little support in learning the English language and American ways. These early immigrants did not have the benefit of bilingual street signs or bilingual education. Many went to school at night to learn the language and customs of this new land called America.

Because the climate and the land itself resembled that of Finland, many of the Finns who came to America in the early 1900s settled in Minnesota and Michigan. Wanting to improve themselves and succeed in this new country, many of these immigrants went to work in the logging industry or in the iron ore mines where they performed hazardous jobs, often for low wages. Above all, many of them wanted to be Americans; thus, they stayed and in their own way helped to build America. Mother, as a cook, laundress, child care worker, ironer, and seamstress, contributed her share to make life fuller and richer for all of those whom she touched.

After her marriage, she devoted herself entirely to making a home for her family. When she and Dad moved to the country in May of 1923, she had four children under the age of six, and she was eight months pregnant. My brother Paul was born barely a month after the move to the country. If Mother had any symptoms of postpartum depression, she kept them to herself. She did not have time to be depressed or to feel sorry for herself. She had four girls and a baby boy who needed care; they were her priorities.

As the summer wore on, we girls suffered through measles and chicken pox. There were times, I am sure, when Mother would have gladly given up her position for one that could have been more rewarding. But the Finnish people are blessed with something the whole world has come to admire. It is called Sisu.

Because it is so uniquely Finnish, there is no English word equivalent to it. Sisu is what Mother and Father had. Sisu is what it took to tackle the rigors of life in the wilderness—with nothing but their two hands to help them.

Mother's hands were always busy, whether they were holding a baby, crocheting, knitting, turning a hay rake, or kneading a batch of bread dough. She relaxed by being busy. If she went to a neighbor's she took her work along. She had a pink-and-tan tapestry bag with wooden handles; in it she kept half-done pieces of crocheting, a half-knit woolen stocking, or perhaps a flour-sack pillowcase waiting to be embroidered. Whatever it was, she took the bag with her and kept her hands busy while she exchanged neighborhood news and gossip with her friends.

Mother was very creative in many ways. If she saw a picture of a garment she particularly liked, she was able to reproduce it for one or all of us girls. She never needed a pattern; she trusted her memory and her sense of style to make clothes for us. Even when we were in high school in Ely and were not at home to try them on, she made blouses and skirts that fit perfectly.

One of my most vivid memories of Mother's creativity was in the spring of 1928. It had been a long cold winter. The whole family was ready for warmer weather. When we came home from school that afternoon, Mother sent Martha to the playhouse to get a piece of meat for supper. (For lack of a better place, our playhouse was used as a deep-freeze during the winter months.)

When Martha did not return as expected, Mother sent Esther to find out what was taking Martha so long. When Esther failed to return, Mother sent Ora and me to hurry the girls along. Imagine our surprise when we stepped inside to see the transformation which had taken place. Mother had spent the better part of the day—when she was not nursing my baby sister, Elsie—cleaning the playhouse for us. Not only had she put clean curtains in the windows, but she had also wallpapered the entire place, using the sample pages from the many wallpaper catalogs that arrived each spring. It was beautiful by any standards, and we could hardly wait for summer vacation to come.

Then there was the Christmas when each of us received a new doll. Martha's doll was named Mabel, Esther's was Nellie, and mine was Kitty. Kitty was a beautiful doll with a head of deep, brown hair. Dolls' hair in those days was not rooted like many of today's dolls. Instead, the hair was pasted to a scalp piece which was in turn glued to the back of the doll's head. After countless brushings and combings, Kitty was quite bald. But that did not faze Mother; she got busy with Dad's awl and some black cotton thread and created a new look for Kitty. Using the original scalp piece, she punched holes with the awl, and proceeded to tie loops of the black thread through it to give Kitty a new hair-do. The result was truly what could be called "stringy" hair, but I loved Kitty anyway. To me, she was still a beautiful doll. It is little things like this I remember most fondly. Even though Mother was not often openly demonstrative with her feelings, we knew she loved us.

DAD

Dad, Paul (Paavo) Kaurala, was born in Kiuruvesi, Finland, on October 1, 1888. When he was twenty-five years of age, he decided to leave his childhood home and come to America to seek new opportunities. When he left Finland, he promised his father he would be back in three years to remove some stumps remaining from trees he and his younger brother, Robert, had cut down. The three years were to stretch out to become fifty-four before he returned to Finland.

Dad arrived in Montreal, Canada, in 1913 with not much more than the clothes on his back. On his first night in Montreal, he was walking along a street with a fellow shipmate when he was aware he was being followed by a police officer. He and his friend ducked into a tavern to avoid any trouble, only to find the lawman following them into the bar. By this time, Dad and his friend were terrified to be followed thus by the police, wondering what law they had broken.

Fortunately, the bartender knew enough Finnish and English to clarify the situation for the new immigrants. The policeman explained to the bartender, who in turn explained to Dad, that he admired Dad's handmade Finnish boots, and wanted to buy them.

Needless to say, no deal was made. The boots were the only

4

pair of shoes Dad owned, and he was not about to start his new life in his bare feet.

Shortly after his arrival in Montreal, Dad found employment in the logging industry. The following year, he crossed the border into Minnesota, where he again worked as a logger. By late 1914 he found his way to Ely, where he held various jobs before going to work in the iron ore mines.

Dad continued to work in the underground mines until the late 1920s. He was injured several times. I can still remember the night he came home with a large bandage covering his forehead. He had cut his head on a steel beam, and the company doctor had treated him. We were so concerned about his injury. When the bandages came off, and we saw the metal staples or clips which had been used to close the gash, we thanked God the injury was not more serious. Mother was a bit inclined to blame Dad; she always believed carelessness was the cause of most accidents.

There are many memories of those years when Dad worked at the iron ore mines. He had a quaint, oval-shaped tin lunchbox which consisted of two layers. The bottom layer was for his tea, and the upper layer was for his sandwiches and other foods. During the week, when he stayed in Ely, he lived at a rooming house with fellow miners. He often told the story of how he antagonized his landlady with his droll sense of humor.

It seems that each of the men had their favorite tools. They would hurry out of the dining hall after a meal and make a mad scramble for the best tools. Once, when the men were on a lunch-break, Dad took his pickax into the dining hall. When Dad showed up in the dining hall, carrying a pickax, his fellow miners asked him why he had done this. Dad, always ready with a quick remark, replied, "I thought I'd be prepared, in case the pie crust is tough." Naturally, this got back to his landlady, who was quite perturbed until Dad explained the real reason for bringing the pickax into the dining hall.

Another vivid memory of Dad's mining years is the foul-smelling carbide lamp which he wore on his forehead. It was a little canister with a reflector in the back. Dad filled the canister with the white carbide substance. When water was added to it, a gas was produced which burned brightly for several hours. In the mine pits, this was the only illumination, and if the flame went out unexpectedly the miners were at each other's mercy.

Dad's transportation to and from Ely must have posed quite the problem during those years. We had no car and no telephone to arrange car-pooling with other miners, and—worst of all—we lived on a very bad gravel road. Most of the time Dad would leave home on foot. If he was lucky, he would manage to be picked up by a kind-hearted motorist who took him the rest of the way to Ely. Very often, on his return home on a Saturday, some of his friends in Ely brought him and spent the remainder of the weekend with us.

It was in the summer of 1927 when Dad bought his first car, and I will never forget how proud we were to think we actually owned a car! It was a Ford touring car which had seen better days. The canvas side-curtains, with their cracked celluloid windows, were not much protection from the elements, but we did not mind. The important thing was that we were no longer stuck on the farm.

That summer, we had a hired man named John helping Dad to clear the land, make fences, and perform the countless other chores around the farm. John also took upon himself the task of teaching Dad to drive. When Dad went to Ely to take his driver's exam, we girls were on pins and needles until Dad came home, having passed his test.

The bullies in school quickly gave our car a nickname. They called it Kaurala's Piss-Pot, a label which caused us much heartache. (Incidentally, some of those same bullies were only too happy to accept a ride in the car!) "Piss-Pot" or Ford, the name did not matter; we had many years and many miles of pleasant memories as we enjoyed the freedom that car ownership provided us. When Dad junked the car years later, some of the neighborhood young men wanted to buy it. Dad refused, however, because he had legally "killed" it through the Department of Motor Vehicles.

Our next car was another open-air touring car—a great big Nash which boasted a huge engine. We had this car until 1932 or so, at which time Dad bought a closed sedan. The car was made by

Continental Motors, a company that went the way of many of the early car makers. The *DeVaux*, as it was called, was a big improvement over the touring cars we had owned previously. It was more dependable, even in cold weather. For once we did not have to worry about getting wet if we happened to be on the road when a sudden shower came up.

Dad continued to buy previously-owned cars until after World War II, when he purchased his first *new* car, a yellow Ford pick-up truck. He owned several other new cars and continued to drive until just after his eightieth birthday. Dad's driving privileges came to a grinding halt when he "borrowed" my brother Paul's new truck to drive to the store, about ten miles away. He had only gone a little over a mile when he was struck by a huge truck, and forced off the ice-covered road. Fortunately, Dad suffered only minor injuries, but Paul's truck did not escape damage. When Paul came home from work that afternoon, Dad met him at the door saying, "I was a bad boy today, and I broke your new truck." Amused as Paul was by Dad's confession, he nevertheless decided it was time for Dad to surrender his license.

From the time we were old enough to understand, we knew our everyday behavior was subject to Mother's discipline. However, if Mother's admonitions went unheeded, Dad stepped in. He never said much, he did not have to. Most of the time, all it took was a stern look in our direction, and we knew he meant business. He had two horizontal lines in the middle of his forehead—right between his eyes. We called them his *vihasia*, or "angry marks." As soon as they appeared, we put a stop to any unacceptable behavior.

Among other things, Dad was a highly skilled carpenter. In his later years he built many homes in the Babbitt area. Even after he had officially retired, he kept himself busy by building or remodeling homes, building cabinets, and making various items in his woodworking shop. He was close to seventy when he and Mother built a cottage at Bear Island Lake near Babbitt, Minnesota. The little cabin and the nearby sauna represented Mother's dream-come-true. She had always hoped for a place by the lake, nestled among the white birches and the quiet waters. She would sit for hours on the landing dock, enjoying the evening solitude. They even bought a small boat. Mother and Dad would often spend quiet hours rowing around the lake, communing with nature.

Dad had a soft spot which most people never knew existed. He loved cats with a passion, and he always had one around. To hear him and the cat carry on a conversation was truly remarkable. One of his favorites was a gray cat named Eva. She lived to be quite old. She and Dad understood each other very well. When Dad went into the barn, Eva always came running up to him, invariably complaining about something—at least Dad interpreted it as complaining. If Eva was not cold, she was hungry, tired, or the cows were abusing her. Whenever Eva had kittens, she would trust no one but Dad to come near her. She was truly devoted to him and forgave him even after he gave her kittens away.

Throughout his adult years, Dad dreamed of going back to Finland to, as he put it, "remove the stumps" he had left behind when he came to America. But with a large family to feed and clothe, along with the many other demands of the farm, he had to be content with only the dreams of his childhood home. When Mother passed away in 1965, Dad decided it was time to go back, and in August of the following year he took me with him to see the fulfillment of a fifty-four-year-old dream.

We flew from Duluth International Airport on the second of August aboard a four-engine, *Finnair* plane, with some eighty other passengers. We arrived at the Helsinki Airport in the early hours of the third of August. After the mass confusion of the first half-hour at the air terminal, Dad and I found ourselves to be the only people there, except for two other men who seemed to be looking for someone. I nudged Dad, suggesting those two just *might* be looking for him, but he shushed me up, saying, "My brother isn't *that* old." Poor Dad did not realize how fifty-four years had changed his brother from a young teenager into an old man.

After the two brothers were reunited, we left the airport and headed for Uncle Bob's house. One of the first sights we saw as we drove through Helsinki was a huge billboard reading, *"Pankaa Tiikeri Tankkiin."* It was the Esso Tiger, with the well-known slogan "Put a Tiger in Your Tank." This, and several other definitely American advertisements, caused Dad much disappointment. He had expected Finland to have stood still all those years. Instead, he found a Finland which was modern in every respect. It was not until we went to Kiuruvesi, his childhood village, that he felt he had truly come home.

We spent six weeks in Finland, and I have always felt that Dad was never the same afterward. Maybe he thought his lifelong dream was fulfilled, and he had nothing more to look forward to; he had very little zest for life after returning to Minnesota. When I last saw him in August of 1971, he said God had him on "overtime." He was ready to join Mother, but had to wait until she was ready for him. His health failed gradually that winter. He spent his last year in a nursing home, where he passed away in early December of 1972, a few months into his eighty-fifth year.

It is strange, after all these years, that memories such as these come to mind. As I recall certain incidents, they remind me of other things which are not necessarily related. Above all, the memories tell of an understood love. I do not recall Father ever telling me he loved me. Yet I know he loved us, each and all, in his own way. He taught us to love one another, and to live by the Golden Rule—to do unto others as you would want them to do unto you.

THE EARLY YEARS

"For living quarters, he purchased an old,
two-room-plus attic house, which was hauled
to the site by horses."

MEMORIES

My earliest memories go back to the house we rented in Ely, Minnesota, in 1922. I was about three and a half years old at the time. Mother and Dad had been married a few years and, so far, had been blessed with four daughters. Martha, the oldest, had arrived on April 13, 1917; Esther, the next to come, was born on May 10, 1918; and I, the third child, first saw the light on Halloween night, 1919. Then on Thanksgiving Day, 1921, my sister Ora was born. I can well imagine the frustration my father must have felt as each daughter appeared on the scene; in those days many fathers dreamed of having sons to carry on the family name.

During the early years money was tight, so Mother made most of our underwear out of flour sacks. Sometimes she was unable to remove the printed label before she sewed the garments. We often had *Pillsbury Best* on our back-side or across the front of a petticoat. Sometimes it was *Dakota Maid* or *Very Best Occident*.

My earliest recollections are of sitting cross-legged on the bare floor of the kitchen. I sat there, naked except for my *Pillsbury Best* bloomers, awaiting my turn in the round galvanized laundry tub to have my Saturday night bath. Mother performed this task assembly-line fashion, starting with Martha, and giving us each a good shampoo and scrubbing.

Why would an ordinary, Saturday night bath be so well-remembered? Because there I was, practically naked, when a delivery boy came in carrying Mother's groceries. It wasn't merely the fact that he arrived just then, but he had caught me, literally, with my foot in my mouth. To a three year old, putting a foot in the mouth is a relatively simple matter, but when he remarked, "That girl is eating her toes," it became a laughing matter. For months afterward, whenever I saw that rosy-cheeked, blond-haired delivery boy, I wanted to crawl into a hole. I have always had my own very special meaning of the expression "putting a foot in your mouth."

For the weekly Saturday night baths, the laundry tub was placed on two kitchen chairs in front of the wood-burning range. Mother kept the oven door open so the room would be warm for this weekly ritual. Bathtubs were scarce in the homes of this era. Most families at this time had no bathroom as such; indoor plumbing came much later. The beginning of the modern bathroom was merely a "throne" in an empty closet or convenient nook. As a young child, I remember the throne as a dark closet with a bare light bulb hanging from the ceiling. The toilet was the main feature, with the water closet high up on the wall with a pull-chain to operate the flusher.

The Finnish people, however, had their special way for keeping clean. There was usually a neighborhood sauna where whole families went to enjoy the rituals of a real Finnish bath. There were many Finnish sauna baths in most of the Iron Range towns where the population was predominantly Finnish. Most of the saunas were built of hand-hewn logs, with neatly dovetailed corners. There were two rooms: a dressing and undressing room and the sauna proper. The large stone fireplace, or *kiuas*, was the main feature of the room. The fire was started several hours beforehand so that the round stones on top were heated through. The *löyly*, or steam, was created when a dipperful of water was thrown on the hot stones. Most of the saunas had a system of coiled pipes in the firebox; water was heated as it circulated through the pipes into a holding tank next to the kiuas.

Whenever possible, Mother and Dad took us to the neighbor's

sauna. Mother washed us, one at a time, in a laundry tub or galvanized pail. Dad acted as receiver, as each freshly washed girl was handed to him in the dressing room. Usually, he dressed us in our clean, white flannel nightgowns and lined us up on the long bench where we sat quietly while he and Mother had their sauna. Then they bundled us up to take us home, with Martha and Esther walking and Ora and I being carried. Later on, when we moved to the country, one of the first priorities—after the house and the "outhouse" were built—was the building of the sauna.

In May of 1923, Mother and Dad decided to move their growing family to rural Babbitt, where Dad had purchased some land several years previously. The home site was a small clearing in the middle of a wilderness. Dad had spent some time cutting trees and brush to provide a place for the house. As time passed, he and Mother worked to clear the land to make room for the out-buildings and a small garden plot. I can remember very clearly some summer weekends in 1923 and 1924 when friends from Ely came to help Dad with the land-clearing. Gradually, we had enough open land to provide pasture for several cows, as well as a field that could be planted to yield winter feed for the animals.

For living quarters, Dad purchased an old, two-room-plus-attic house, which was hauled to the site by horses. The little house was bug-infested and not exactly Mother's dream home. Nevertheless, she was determined to make the best of it.

The bedbugs were a problem for the first year or so; they crawled out through the seams in the old wallpaper. Every Saturday, Mother stripped the beds and, using a rag saturated with kerosene, wiped the coil springs of the beds. Then she took a small triangle-shaped box of *Watkins Bedbug Powder* and proceeded to dust the mattresses, being careful to dust every corner and under the seams. Her efforts paid off, and within the year the bedbugs disappeared.

The first few weeks in our new surroundings were full of discoveries and incredible wonders for us. We had a yard that had no limits, and the land, as far as our eyes could see, was our very own!

June brought with it new wonders—the first wild strawberries of the season. Every morning the four of us, Martha, Esther, Ora, and I, covered our heads with dishtowels to protect us from sun and insects. Then, with each of us carrying a cup or bowl, we were off into the nearby woods to pick the sweet, wild berries. We went alone, without Mother. Mother was in her ninth month of pregnancy, and she could easily see us from the house. Besides, there was a big, dark spruce tree that we used as our landmark. We never worried about getting lost, because whenever we saw the big tree, we knew we were close to home.

It was on one of our berry-picking excursions that I decided to fill my cup with something that was much more plentiful and easier to pick. I was very proud to present Mother with a cup brimming full of little, round, brown nuggets. In reply to my question, *"Mitä mannuja nämä on?"* which, translated means, "What berries are these?" Mother calmly answered, *"Ne on Jänneksen mannuja, älä niitä syö,"* which means "Those are Rabbit Berries, don't eat them." I had filled my cup with rabbit poop.

THE BLUE FLIES

In the summer of 1924, while the kitchen was being built, the days were filled with confusion and commotion. The original two-room house was now almost doubled in size, and the huge kitchen was the most lived-in part of the house. We even had a white porcelain sink and a little red pump which would provide water—a huge step forward in modernization. What progress we had made from a water well—where a winch would lower a bucket into the well to bring up the water—to the convenience of an indoor pump. Even though there were times when the pump would fail and the water had to be carried in, we nevertheless felt quite lucky with our modern facilities.

The sink drain, however, was another story. It was not hooked up until much later. For the time being, a "slop-pail" was used. In the late 1920s and early 1930s, septic systems as such were not very common. Most homes had a slop pail under the sink for collecting dishwater, leftover coffee, and nighttime emergencies when a trip to the outhouse was out of the question. The slop pail was carried out and emptied several times a day, usually near the barnyard. Dad eventually dug a deep trench from the cellar door to the barnyard and put in a heavy iron pipe to handle the drainage from the kitchen sink. Even though the drain took care of the waste water from the kitchen, the slop pail was still kept for emergencies.

While the confusion of the kitchen construction was going on, I was quite content to sit outside on the slanting cellar door. There I would sit for hours, watching the big, shiny blue flies buzzing aimlessly around. The sight of their bright-blue bodies, covered with prickly hairs, fascinated me and kept me occupied for hours.

A few years later, the cellar entrance was moved to the kitchen end of the house. My cellar door spot in the sun was gone forever. But the blue flies live on.

ROSIE THE COW AND OTHER COWS

In 1924, Mother and Dad decided we needed a cow. With our growing family, milk was a necessity. Even though a cow was a huge responsibility, she would be worth her weight, if not in gold, then in milk, cream and butter. By spring we had acquired a cow. She provided milk, cream and butter as long as we provided for her during the long, cold winter which usually lasted from mid-October to the end of May.

Our new cow, Rosie, was red and white and of questionable parentage, but to us she was a treasure. Dad built a small log barn before Rosie came. Knowing that at some future date he planned to buy more cows, Dad built two stanchions in the barn, plus a space for a calf or two. Stanchions were partitions in the barn. To make it easier to feed and milk them, each cow was chained to her own stanchion. Modern barns do not have partitions, because milking machines require easy access to the cows, among "udder" things.

One afternoon during a severe thunderstorm, we heard loud noises in the barn. Because of the storm we ignored the sounds, and they were soon forgotten. When Mother went to the barn some hours later to do the evening milking she was horrified to see that Rosie had hung herself in her stall. She had apparently tried to turn around in the stall and got tangled in her chain.

With the help of a neighbor, Dad managed to drag Rosie's body out of the barn. She was buried in a peaceful, quiet place in the meadow. For years, we gathered wild flowers to make wreaths for Rosie's grave. As the years passed, we witnessed the arrival and departure of many cows. I remember some of them very well: Moolie, Hertta, Onnenkukka, Mansu, Rusina, and Augusta to name a few.

Much of my early sex education can be attributed to the cows. Every so often, a cow was "ready for the bull," and since we did not have a bull, we took the cow to the neighbor's. I was often "drafted" to help drive the cow to the bull. In my seven- or eight-year-old mind, I had no idea of what it was all about. I can still hear the lady, the owner of the bull, saying, "Sampo, jump!" On the way home, walking behind the cow, I could not help but wonder about the blood-tinged, sticky liquid dripping from under the cow's tail. When we got home, Dad took the calendar from the wall and marked a date nine months into the future. It just did not make sense to me.

Cows played many a part in our growing-up years. During the bleakness of the Depression, about 1932, we were facing what would have been the saddest Christmas for us all. There was no work for Dad, and no prospects for work in the near future. We were by then a family of nine, the last two having arrived in 1927 and 1929. Esther was in the seventh grade and I was in sixth. Although we dreamed of having new dresses for the Christmas program, we knew it was probably not to be.

Out of the cold, on a crisp, wintry Sunday morning, there was a knock on the door. When Mother answered it, a man came in, asking to buy a cow. Since we had more cows than we needed and there was no market for milk, Mother and Dad knew what they must do. They sold their best milk cow for the magnificent sum of thirty-five dollars. That thirty-five dollars made the difference between a bleak Christmas and a happy one for us all. Esther and I got our new dresses from the Chicago Mail Order House for $1.98 each. Esther's dress was a lovely turquoise color which, unfortunately, fume-faded by spring. Mine was a pretty coral shade, and I wore it for "best" for a long time.

BLUEBERRIES AND OTHER DELIGHTS

Toward the end of July each year, the whole family went on a blueberry-picking expedition. Mother always packed a lunch, because we left as soon as the morning milking was done and did not return until it was time for the evening milking. My favorite picking place was at a farm in White Iron. Friends of Dad's owned the area and were generous in allowing our family to pick berries there.

When we arrived at the berry field, Dad went off by himself, leaving Mother with her brood of children. Mother was rather limited as far as mobility was concerned; she usually had a baby to nurse—Paul until he was three, then Elsie, who was weaned earlier because Lauri was on the way, and Lauri, who was not weaned until three and a half. So Mother stayed near the baby while the rest of us scattered to find a good place to pick.

Martha, being the oldest, was also the boldest. She went off alone, and was always scanning the bushes ahead to find better pickings. Esther, on the other hand, found a spot to pick and remained there until she was satisfied that it was picked clean. Ora and I often picked together; because of her poor vision she could not see the berries too well. She had a habit of trampling the bushes and ruining the berries. Because she was small, she wanted to stay close to me so she would not get lost. Invariably, she would get separated from me and spill her berries in her haste to find me. I had a five-pound lard pail to pick into, and she had a small tin cup. Whenever she filled her cup, she poured it into my pail.

By the time we were ready to go home, we had filled the two five-gallon milk cans, plus the lard pails. For the next two days, we were kept busy picking over the berries, and Mother was busy canning them. Mother usually had about forty quarts of blueberries stashed away for the winter. Having a sweet, juicy blueberry pie in the middle of January somehow helped to make the winter more bearable.

Mother's stock of goodies in the cellar included many other Minnesota fruits. She had quarts and quarts of wild strawberries which we girls painstakingly gathered. As the long summer progressed, there were wild pin cherries, red raspberries, and chokecherries to pick. Mother made wild cherry jelly, the likes of which I have never tasted since. Sometimes she cooked the cherries, strained out the stones, and canned the juice. In the winter, she cooked the juice and added sugar and thickening to make a sauce to serve over baked rice pudding.

Chokecherries were quite plentiful in the area, but for some reason they did not make a satisfactory jelly. So Mother used them to make a syrup which was wonderful on pancakes and French toast.

Rhubarb was another plentiful item in those days. I can remember when Mother was given several rhubarb plants, which we often called "pie plant." In a few years, these plants had multiplied so we had more rhubarb than we needed. So, when we were not busy picking berries or making hay, we were busy washing and cutting rhubarb. Mother canned some of it uncooked and unsweetened, and some she used to make rhubarb-strawberry preserves or rhubarb-orange marmalade. In the winter, when we had marmalade sandwiches in our lunch pails, we never had trouble making a trade with one of our classmates, who would gladly exchange a half of an apple for one of our sandwiches.

The garden often yielded a bumper crop of goodies for Mother's cellar shelves. Sweet cucumber pickles, green tomato pickles, and pickled beets provided a welcome addition to the humdrum menus of the Depression years.

Then there were the canned string and wax beans. Mother canned them as fast as they appeared in the garden. One of our favorite meals was creamed green beans on toast. Mother often prepared this for our lunch on Saturdays, when she had to come up with a meal to satisfy five or six hungry children.

When the carrots were harvested in the fall, Dad buried them in a wooden barrel filled with sand. The carrots kept fresh through the winter, eliminating the need for Mother to can them. With bushels and bushels of homegrown potatoes in the cellar, we were never too concerned when the cold winds of winter began to blow.

THE WOLF AT THE DOOR

Because Dad was still working at the Mine in Ely, Mother had arranged to have a neighbor girl, Laila, stay with us as a sort of companion and Mother's Helper. She was from a family of eight children and attended the public school with Martha and Esther. Mother taught Laila to sew clothes for herself, as well as for us. Years later, Laila told me how fortunate she had been to stay with us; she still remembered how Mother taught her to cut and fit garments without the use of patterns. Laila was about fourteen years old and, from the beginning, we loved her as we would a big sister.

In the long winter evenings, we sat around the big wooden kitchen table, doing our needle work in the glow of a flickering kerosene light. There was Mother, Laila, Martha, Esther, Ora and myself; each of us had a piece of material on which Mother had stamped a simple design to be worked. Mine was a cross-stitched rose design, which I struggled to embroider.

Ora, a little past three at the time, had not as yet mastered the art of sewing. This did not stop her, however, she merely took her piece of material and by pushing the needle in and out, gathered the fabric into a rosette which she hung on the wall with the needle. The wall paper was full of tiny holes where Ora hung up her handiwork. When Mother wanted a needle she simply removed one of Ora's masterpieces from the wall. For years afterward, Mother remembered how Ora planted needles on the walls. The flickering kerosene light which lit those evening gatherings was not the ideal illumination for embroidery work, but nevertheless we spent many happy hours stitching and chatting.

One evening, as we sat there, we heard the unmistakable

howling of a wolf. It sounded very close, so we climbed upstairs to look. When we looked out of the window, there, bathed in moonlight, was a huge wolf! As we watched, he raised his head and howled a sad, mournful cry. As he did so, every hair on our heads stood up, and every inch of skin felt cold and crawly. We watched him for what seemed like hours, until he finally gave up and went to seek newer, more promising horizons.

For weeks after that, we were reluctant to go to the outhouse by ourselves. But gradually, as the winter wore on and the wolf did not reappear, we got over our fears and things were back to normal. To this day, whenever I hear the expression "wolf at the door," I am reminded of this experience.

THE OFFICE BUILDING
(THE FAMILY ROOM)

Every farm had an "office building." This building had many names, such as "the place," "the privy," "the john," or "the two-holer." It was usually built near the barn, possibly so that the odors would mingle with the manure heap odors, and thus be less offensive. Commonly, there were two holes: the larger one was for the parents and teenagers and the smaller hole was for the kids. Disposable diapers had not been invented yet, so kids had to learn to use the john by the time they were two.

In the summer months a trip to the privy was quite routine. But during the cold weather, in the endless months of winter, it could be quite an ordeal. For this reason, Mother always kept a kerosene lantern hanging on a nail in the porch off the kitchen. The lantern served many purposes: it lit the way from the main house to the outhouse and back, it provided heat while we were heeding nature's call, and it made it possible to select the right pages from the Sears' or Ward's catalog for the wiping-up process. Selecting the proper pages was very important. We learned quite early in life that the yellow pages were much more effective wipers than the glossy, colored pages. The colored pages had a tendency to slide—this created problems, particularly if one had a slight case of diarrhea.

Another problem with the outhouse was insects. In the summer months, multitudes of insects, from the tiniest no-see-ums to the big, hard-shelled beetles found their way into the outhouse. Wasps and hornets attacked without warning. More than once Dad was stung on a very delicate part of his anatomy while he was seated on the throne.

Chipmunks, mice, and rats often found their way into the building. Dad had once hung his carpenter's apron on a nail in the outhouse. Two days later, a mouse had built her nest in the pocket. Imagine Dad's surprise when he reached into the pocket for a nail!

The two-holer served its purpose for many years. After World War II, when rural electrification came to the area, many of the outdoor privies disappeared. Although indoor toilets are more convenient and sanitary, they lack the togetherness that was a part of the little house by the barn. There, one could spend time daydreaming or sharing an intimate moment with a sister or girlfriend. Many facts of life were passed on behind the door of the office. In many ways, this little house was like the family room of today.

A SON IS BORN

On the morning of June 22, 1924, Dad hustled us off to pick strawberries a little earlier than usual. When we returned, around noon, he met us at the door. He was holding a naked, red, screaming bundle of *boy*—our baby brother! Naturally, we were amazed, because there was no doctor with his black bag, and certainly there was no evidence of a stork hovering nearby. In answer to our questions of "where" and "how come?" Dad seriously replied, "In the carrot patch." We truly believed him and accepted his explanation. For some time afterward, we were reluctant to eat a carrot with a double root, because we actually believed the two roots were the beginnings of legs of a baby. Occasionally, we found a carrot with two roots and a third, a tiny one, which we thought was the start of a baby boy.

After a few weeks, the thrill of having a baby brother began to fade. He was a very demanding baby. It took only a few whimpers on his part, and Mother was making a hasty retreat to the bedroom, bosom exposed, to nurse him. As older sisters, we felt this young king threatened us with his presence. It seemed he not only got the lion's share of attention, but, literally, the lion's share of everything else.

As he grew and thrived, things went from bad to worse. Mealtime conversations usually revolved around the differences between girls' (ours) and boys' (his) nutritional requirements. In those days, it was almost an established fact that growing boys required more meat and desserts than did growing girls. We quickly learned to be satisfied with a fatty piece of meat or a smaller cut of pie. At the time, sons were often seen as more important than girls as future labor on the farms. After all, it was assumed our brother would one day be Dad's main help on the farm. Yet, it would be years before Dad could count on help from his son. In the meantime, there was work to be done on the farm.

FARM CHORES

"Esther was seven years of age and I not quite six
when we learned to rake the alfalfa
and clover into stacks, to be later
carried into the barn loft."

CHILD LABOR

Dad's work at the Pioneer Mine in Ely kept him away from home most of the week. Thus, on his days off, he worked seventeen or eighteen hours a day clearing land, plowing, planting and doing the countless other tasks that needed to be done. While he waited for his son to grow up, he had to rely on his girls. We were introduced to the working end of a hay rake years before the term "child labor" was in our vocabulary. Esther was seven years of age and I not quite six when we learned to rake the alfalfa and clover into stacks, to be later carried into the barn loft.

Dad cut the alfalfa by hand, using a scythe. All these years later, I can still see him swinging the scythe through the field, watching the wind-rows form as he rhythmically swished the shiny, wicked-looking blade from right to left. Every so often he stopped to sharpen the blade with a whet-stone he carried in his pocket. At the end of the day, he gave the scythe a complete going over on the huge grindstone by the well. Martha and I took turns at the crank, while Esther had the task of pouring water on the grindstone. Later on, Dad made a treadle type control for the wheel, and he attached a tin can to a long pole on the frame of the grindstone. When he needed water on the stone, all he had to do was pull a string; the can would tilt, pouring just enough water to provide the moisture needed for the task.

Two days after the alfalfa was cut, our job was to turn the wind-rows to allow the hay to dry. If the weather held, by afternoon the hay was ready to be taken into the barn. With the four of us—Ora, Esther, Martha, and myself—working as a well-trained team, we managed to get the hay gathered. Dad had made a litter-like contraption about six feet long with cross bars placed as needed to provide a sturdy base. With Martha and Ora at one end and Esther and I at the other, we carried load after load of hay into the loft. This was true kid power, and we did not expect to be paid for it. We knew it was work that had to be done. We also knew the work on the farm would not get done by itself.

CHORES

Mother and Dad were firm believers in assigning each of us chores to do on a regular schedule. My first chore, when I was four years of age, was the woodbox. Every Saturday morning I was to empty it, sweep, and refill it. The front of the box was hinged to facilitate the sweeping-out process. I used to prop the front up with a piece of wood while I was sweeping. But one day, the prop was knocked out by the broom handle, and I saw the entire solar system when the heavy front came crashing across the bridge of my nose.

For weeks afterward, my nose was swollen and painful inside and out. It may have been broken, but one did not go running to the doctor unless someone was dead or dying. However, Dad did fix a hook-and-eye latch to the woodbox front so that when it was Ora's job to clean the woodbox, she didn't risk getting her nose smashed.

When I outgrew the woodbox chore, I graduated to the stair-well pantry duty. This, too, had to be done every week. Everything had to come off the shelves, the shelves and floor had to be scrubbed, and then everything was returned to its place. I always enjoyed doing the pantry because all the interesting things were kept there. The coffee grinder and coffee beans were on the top shelf; boxes of kitchen matches and Parowax on the next shelf. The third shelf held an assortment of things such as burned candles from birthday cakes and Christmas and, perhaps, a few empty Mason jars. On the top shelf, next to the coffee grinder, Mother usually kept a yellow box of *Domino* sugar lumps. Whenever I had a chance, I would sneak a lump or two to satisfy my sweet tooth.

The Mason jars were not always empty. One jar usually held scraps of soaps which Mother melted down to use in the laundry. There were so many beautiful colors: the light green *Palmolive*, a strong lemon-scented yellow soap, and a pretty pink *Watkins Rose Soap*. I remember once when I could not resist the temptation to snatch a few of these lovely colored soaps. I didn't have a pocket on my clothing, so I did the next best thing —I stashed them in my bloomers. All was fine until I sat down, and the lemon soap worked its way up to a very delicate part of my body. I never forgot the sting.

On the floor of the pantry was the huge tinned bowl Mother used for making bread. Next to it was the churn which Dad had made. Later on, Ora and I would spend many an hour taking turns pushing the dasher up and down, waiting for the butter to "come."

Also taking up part of the floor in the pantry were Mother's boxes of carpet rags. There was a box of rags waiting to be cut into strips, and a box or two of round balls of rags ready to be woven into rugs on Mother's loom. Without appearing too obvious about it, I surveyed the fabric contents of the first box to find something that I particularly liked to make something for my dolls. Mother had an uncanny sense of knowing whenever a piece of fabric was missing and usually reclaimed it before I had time to sew a dress for my doll. Later on, when Mother moved the carpet rags into the small shed by the garage, the boxes no longer held the fascination for me, and Mother's carpet rags were safe.

Ironing clothes for a family as big as ours could have become a problem, but Mother, in her usual wisdom, solved the problem before it arose. From the time we were strong enough to lift the heavy cast iron sad-irons from the hot stove, we each had our own pile of ironing to do. As with the laundry, we started learning to iron by doing the handkerchiefs; as we became more proficient, we graduated to pillow cases and dish towels, bed sheets and, finally, to ironing our own dresses.

By the time I was fourteen, Mother depended on me to iron the curtains whenever they were laundered. Nothing was permanent press in those days; every curtain was made of cotton scrim or voile, which required starching and ironing. Later on, Mother had lace curtains in her living room. These did not require ironing, as they were dried on the curtain stretchers which Dad had made. The curtain stretchers were simply rectangular wooden frames, adjustable in width and length to accommodate any size curtain. There were small nails all along the frame so the wet curtains could be tacked to the frame. Then, when the lace curtains were dry, they were carefully peeled off the nails. I used to wish that the ruffled, kitchen curtains could be done on stretchers, but the ruffles made it impossible. So I ironed them.

Still on the chore of ironing, it was quite an undertaking with puffed sleeves, ruffles, sashes and peplums on most of our dresses. There was one thing I have never missed since those days, the mini-pleated organdy frill which was so popular. It was beautiful when it was new, but after laundering it was merely a limp, unattractive evil which, no matter how I tried, I could never get to look the way it did when it was new. Then there was the ric-rac that was used on most of Mother's aprons and house dresses. No matter how I tried to iron them, the points invariably turned down, and the fabric puckered between the rows of ric-rac. But in spite of the problems I encountered in my ironing, I always enjoyed seeing the results of my labors.

Esther loved to peel the potatoes each evening for our supper. For a family as large as ours, it took quite a few potatoes. Esther made the task more pleasant by cutting off a sample of each potato; if she found a particularly tasty one, she set it aside for later. Sometimes she had two or three peeled potatoes in her secret cache, which she would hide until such a time as was convenient for her. Raw potatoes were one of her passions. Her potato-sampling habit continued throughout her life, though she no longer saved the slices for later.

As we grew older, the chores became more difficult. By the time I was eight and Esther was nine, we scrubbed the huge kitchen floor every Saturday morning. Working side-by-side, each taking half of the room, it was almost a pleasure watching the varnished shine reappear after the dirt was removed. Even though there were times when we felt that Mother was pushing us a bit too hard, we have often thanked her for giving us such high standards of housekeeping. When I clean my no-wax floors today or vacuum my soil-resistant carpet, I think of Mother and of how hard she had to work just to make her house livable. If we had not had our chores to do, she would not have had time to be a Mother.

SUNDAY'S REWARD

In doing our haying chores, we had an ulterior motive. We knew that when Dad came home on Saturday night he would be happy to see that the hay was in. Then on Sunday morning, after the cow was milked, Mother would pack the old wicker picnic basket, and we would all pile into Mr. Kuoppala's car, a friend of Dad's from Ely, to head for Birch Lake for the day.

Family and friends relaxing on a Sunday Afternoon in Babbitt, Minn. 1924.

After what seemed like hours, we finally arrived at Jack's place at the lake. Mother spread a blanket for Baby Paul on a shady place near the beach. We girls gathered some large stones to build a make-shift fireplace while Dad cut a couple of sturdy limbs to make a support for the stew pot. Grilled hamburgers and hotdogs had not yet become standard picnic fare. Fish stew, or *kala keittö* as it is known in the Finnish language, was the preferred picnic menu—especially if it was made from the fish we caught that day. After the fireplace was ready and enough firewood gathered, Dad went off to a special spot to try to hook a few perch or pike for the stew. (Mother, who always believed in being prepared for any emergency, usually had a can or two of salmon in the picnic basket, just in case.)

While Baby Paul gurgled and cooed on his blanket, Mother peeled potatoes and onions for the stew. We girls removed our shoes and long, camel-hair tan stockings and went wading, very gingerly at first, then gradually going in deeper and deeper, holding our skirts up as we dodged the waves. Before long, we removed our dresses, then our slips, and we were in our vests and bloomers. The vests were a very essential part of clothing. They provided dressing for the upper torso and provided a convenient place to hang the long garters for our stockings.

We splashed and frolicked in the water until Mother called us to help take care of Baby Paul while she attended to the dinner. When it was ready, so were we! We attacked the fish stew as though we had not eaten for a week. Nothing had ever tasted so good. The outdoor air, the lake side, and the hot summer sun had combined to whet our appetites to make any food taste special. The fish stew with Mother's home-made bread and butter, farm milk, and rhubarb pie for dessert was a simple, nourishing fare. If there was harmful cholesterol in it, we were blissfully unaware.

After dinner, we helped Mother take the dishes to the water's edge to remove food remnants before packing them in the picnic basket. Throw-away dishes and soup bowls did not make the scene until some years later. Then she nursed Baby Paul and rocked him as she sang to him in Finnish, *"Pikku pojan pallerusta, tilu lilu lei, kasvatamme hellun, heh-huh-hei,* " a song that had to do with a little boy who would someday grow up to be a lover.

Mother, being of the old school, firmly believed that going swimming soon after a big meal could cause cramps. She was adamant in her refusal to let us enter the water until an hour after we had eaten. So we waited. Meanwhile, my sisters and I played in the sand, gathering clam shells and making sand castles until Mother said it was safe to go back into the water.

Mother joined us in the water, having left Dad with the sleeping baby. Mother had grown up near the Swedish border by the Gulf of Bothnia and felt that she knew her way around water. How we envied her as she dog-paddled her way through the deeper water where we were not allowed to go. She, like us girls, was clad in her recycled knee-length bloomers and cotton vest which she wore in place of a brassiere. Mother's underwear, like ours, was made from Pillsbury flour sacks. In later years, we had home-made bathing suits, but at this period in time everyone went swimming in their underwear.

Soon it was time to go home. The cow was waiting to be milked, and the dog and cat needed to be fed. As soon as we got home, Dad started a fire in the sauna stove. Even though we had spent the better part of the day in the water, the sauna was necessary to remove the fishy smell off our bodies.

Unfortunately, Dad had not prepared us for the agony we felt when we stepped into the hot sauna. The hours of exposure to the burning rays of the sun combined with the wind, water and sand, plus the hot sauna, would have made Old Nick himself squirm. However, after we lathered our bodies, removed the sand from our belly buttons and other crevices, and followed it with a refreshingly cool rinse, we felt quite human again. We were painfully sun-burned, but the events of the day had worn us out, so sleep came quickly in spite of the sunburn.

As the years went by and the Sunday excursions to the lake continued, we would witness many changes. Motor boats appeared on the scene, lake shore cottages and resorts sprang up, and the pristine beauty of the lake shore changed forever.

JERRY AND TOMMY

Jerry and Tommy were our farm work horses. We acquired Jerry from a friend in Section Thirty. His real name was Jerry, but due to Father's mispronunciation of his name, we often called him "George." Whatever his name, we were proud and happy to have him. Even though he had seen his best years before we got him, he gave us many years of faithful service.

Jerry pulled the plough in the spring when Dad did his planting. In the summer, he pulled the mower, the hay-rake, and the hay wagon. In the fall he pulled the cultivator which Dad used to open the rows of potatoes, and in the winter he pulled the clumsy snowplow which Dad had fashioned from heavy, wooden beams.

During hay-making time, we were always happy when the last load of hay was in each night, because then we were allowed to ride on Jerry's back from the hayfield to the barn. Dad lifted us up onto the horse and, if Jerry had any objections, he never let us know it. Sometimes there were three of us on his back, and he walked very cautiously so as not to cause us to fall off.

In the winter, when the weather changed suddenly into a

Father (Paul Kaurala) with horses Jerry and Tommy, Babbitt, Minn. 1930.

howling blizzard, Jerry and Dad came to meet us when we got off the school bus at the corner on highways #21 and #583. How happy we were to see them! Dad had extra blankets in the sleigh, and after we were snugly tucked in, Jerry waded through the deep swirling snow to deliver us safely home.

I will never forget the day Jerry died. He was sick for several days, and although Dad tried to give him medication, he was beyond help. Jerry died in the spring of 1932. Shortly afterwards we acquired Tommy who, like Jerry, had seen better days. Tommy was our main help until 1942 and worked without fail all year round.

I had a very special relationship with Tommy. Whenever possible, I gave him a lump of sugar or a piece of bread. He was very gentle, and his nose felt soft and velvety as he nibbled the treat out of my hand. Once, he accidentally bit my middle finger; after that, I was more careful to put the treat in the palm of my hand, rather than holding it in my fingers.

One day in mid-winter, when there was a slight break in the weather, Dad harnessed Tommy to the heavy sleigh he used when he had to transfer hay from the big loft in the meadow to the barn. I was watching them as they slowly made their way through the soft, slushy snow. Suddenly, Tommy stumbled and fell. Without stopping to put on a coat, I grabbed a piece of bread and ran out into the field hoping to coax Tommy to get up. But Dad said, "Miriam, it's no use. Tommy is dead." I broke down and cried. I had lost a good friend. Tommy was a trouper to the very end.

When my brother Paul came home after World War II, he and Dad decided to switch to tractor power instead of horse power. Paul said he was tired of looking at the back end of a horse, something he had done since he was six or seven years of age. He needed a change of scenery!

1923-1926

The first summer on the farm was memorable not only because of the arrival of Baby Paul, but also, as the summer wore on, each of us girls suffered measles, then chicken pox, and, in

Ora's case, scarlet fever. That must have been a trying time for Mother, alone in the wilderness with a new baby to nurse and four sick girls on her hands. Poor Ora was the worst, and as a result, her eyes were severely damaged by the scarlet fever. It wasn't until she was in second grade that a routine eye examination by the county nurse showed that she was almost blind. Fortunately, the county health service absorbed most of the cost of her glasses. And, as Ora tells it today, the glasses opened up a whole new world for her. She could actually read the blackboard, and was able to copy the lesson assignments which the teacher wrote on the board.

With the opening of school that fall of 1923, Martha and Esther were enrolled at Public School #74 in St. Louis County. Martha was in the second grade and Esther in first. I used to watch for the school bus in the late afternoon, bringing the girls home. In the winter they rode in a horse-drawn sleigh with a little house on top. The children entered the sleigh through a narrow door on the back. Inside there were wooden benches along each side where the children sat knee-to-knee. A small wood or kerosene stove provided the passengers with some warmth while the tiny square windows on each end barely illuminated the dark interior. The big boys took turns feeding logs into the fire to keep the make-shift bus warm. Even though these same big boys teased the younger children mercilessly, they were, nevertheless, quite willing to give up the warm seats by the fire. Sometimes, as the two horses pulled the sleigh through the snow, the older boys would have an exciting ride by standing on the runners and hanging onto the sides of the sleigh. The ride home took the better part of an hour.

One afternoon when the girls came home, Esther had a large kitchen towel wrapped around her head and covering her chin. She had cut her chin quite badly during a game of "Duck, Duck, Goose." The teacher had done her best to give first aid, but it was obvious, as the cut refused to heal, that sutures should have been used. For years Esther had a nasty scar on her chin, reminding us of that day.

Another vivid memory I have of that year was when Martha and Esther were vaccinated. Martha's vaccination caused no problems, but Esther almost lost her arm because of it. One of the big bullies deliberately punched her arm, and caused the vaccination site to bleed. Consequently, it became infected and her entire arm was swollen and feverish for days afterward. The following year when I went to school, Mother and Dad refused to let me be vaccinated. As a result I was not vaccinated until I was a junior in college.

The following autumn, I too was enrolled in school. I was so happy to be able to share the same experiences that my older sisters had. Needless to say, not all of these experiences were happy ones. Many were the times I came home in tears because one of the big boys called me "polliwog." As I look back on those days now, I realize that he was not being cruel or malicious; he was referring to my size. After all, I was not quite five years old when I entered kindergarten, so being called polliwog was quite befitting.

Every Friday afternoon, we students from the Little Room were allowed to go to the Big Room for school meetings and pep rallies. In those days, we called them "yell meetings," and the cheer leader was called the "yell leader." I can still see big Urho Wallin yelling, "Who are we for? We're for seventy-four! Here's the way we spell it: S-E-V-E-N-T-Y—F-O-U-R; and here's the way we yell it, Seventy-four!" I was fascinated, watching the veins sticking out in his neck as he grew red in the face, immersing us in school spirit.

Then, after the "yells" were over, we held a school meeting to plan a fund-raising. Usually, a school dance was slated with a cake and coffee sale as an added inducement. When the night of the big dance finally arrived, the entire student body was expected to attend. Mother was not happy about us attending the dance because it meant being out late at night at such a tender age. She knew it would be after midnight when we got home—not exactly the proper curfew for little girls under ten years of age. Since it was a school function, she reluctantly baked a cake and helped us get ready. The bus picked us up and delivered us back home when the dance was over.

For years, Mother talked about how excited we were when we got home from the dance that night. To us, it was like having attended Cinderella's Ball for an evening. We had never heard dance music before, and we had never seen dancing. Martha was able to give a good interpretation of the Charleston and a fair imitation of the two-step. For weeks we sang snatches of "Marie," "In a Little Spanish Town" and "Whispering While You Cuddle Near Me." We joked over Big Toivo and Little Inga and their dancing. The school dance was truly something to remember. Later, when the whole country was trying to survive the Depression, we didn't have school dances. Instead, Depression-Era dances were held to help out a neighbor facing foreclosure or to provide a helping hand to a family who had lost their possessions in a fire.

Incidentally, we were no longer allowed to attend these dances. Mother apparently thought we had absorbed enough culture to do us until we were more mature.

SCHOOL DAYS

"To Dad, life was a 'learning experience,' and
he truly believed that to quit learning
was to become stagnant and die."

EDUCATION

From the time Martha and Esther started school, books were very much a part of our lives. *The Little Red Hen* was read and re-read so often that now, almost 70 years later, I can still recite it word for word. Later on when "Tom and Betty" books were part of the curriculum, we memorized them as well. In the third grade I became acquainted with Big Bear Dan and Little Bear Ben. They were characters in a book titled, *Workaday Doings on the Farm.* I read the stories about Father Thrift and books in the *Riverside Literature Series.*

Today the importance of reading to children is well-known. It could be considered a disadvantage that as children our parents did not spend time reading to us. They had many demands on their time, and they were very limited in their English skills. However, we were only too happy to read to them; they, in turn, were learning to read and pronounce English words which do not always sound the way they appear. In Finnish, my parents' native language, all letters are pronounced exactly as they appear in a word; there are no silent letters, and the vowels "e," "i," and "u" have only one sound. The vowels "a" and "o" have two sounds. These are conveniently tacked on at the end of the alphabet as ä and ö with diacritical marks used to indicate pronunciation.

When Mother or Dad did read to us, it was in the Finnish language. We had the Finnish *Aapinen*, a basic primary reader, and we had several volumes of Zachary Topelius' stories. This was truly an example of bilingual skills being taught in the home.

Our parents were always very deeply involved in our schoolwork and homework. As far back as I can remember, we sat around the kitchen table after supper with our books and studies. Dad sat at his usual place, the head of the table. With his pipe in his mouth and the Finnish daily, *The Päivälehti*, in his hands, he sat there, ready to help if we needed help. It was not until I was in my second year of high school that I realized he was there for his own self improvement, too. He was learning, right along with us, geography, world history, literature, and science. He learned the dates and battles of the Revolutionary War, the Civil War, and World War I. He learned the different breeds of sheep, cattle, and pigs when we studied agriculture, and he learned hundreds of new words through our vocabulary assignments. To him, life was a "learning experience," and he truly believed that to quit learning was to become stagnant and die.

Dad was also somewhat of a philosopher. He had a unique way with words, and was often called upon to speak at social functions. To me, the best part of his philosophy was expressed when he would wake us up each morning. The words lose some of their luster when translated from the Finnish language, but the sum and substance of it was:

> *"Here is a brand new day for you.*
> *Wake up and see what you can do with it.*
> *Remember, yesterday is gone,*
> *And so are its mistakes.*
> *Today is a new page for you to write.*
> *Make this page as good as you can,*
> *With new hopes and new strengths. "*

When Dad and I went to Finland in 1966, the highlight of the trip was a visit to his mother's and father's graves. He spoke eloquently at the cemetery, pouring out his feelings of sorrow at not having been there earlier; by the time he finished his eulogy, there was not a dry eye in the group of relatives who had gathered.

SCHOOL # 74

Our school was considered superior to many other schools in the area. It had two classrooms with a two-bedroom teacherage upstairs. The Little Room housed grades one through four, and the Big Room housed grades five through eight. As enrollment fluctuated, the arrangement might change, but usually this was the accepted division of classes. Later, a portable building was moved in and placed next to the school proper. Grades seven and eight were housed in the portable. Then in the early 1930s this building was used for the high school.

Because indoor plumbing was unknown in rural areas at this time, a large woodshed-privy building, adjacent to the school, provided the conveniences, while a backyard pump provided water. The girls' toilets were on one side of the building, the woodshed was in the middle, and the boys' toilets were on the other side. Because the big boys had the responsibility of carrying firewood into the school rooms as well as the teacherage, it was not unexpected to see a face peeking down through the air shaft while we were occupying one of the four holes. One of the more enterprising bullies had discovered that a hole could be cut through the woodshed wall. On several occasions, a hand would come up through the wall.

Disposable cups and towels had not yet reached our area, so each child had to provide his own cup and towel. Each Monday we took a clean towel to school, and on Friday we brought it home to be laundered. Mother, always wanting to show that she possessed some nice things, really stuck her neck out when she trusted us with some of her best hem-stitched, monogrammed linen towels. Imagine her reaction when the towels returned on Friday after having been used by the teacher to wipe the blackboards. By the following year, paper towels and waxed paper cups were provided by the school district, so we no longer had to provide our own cups and towels.

Frozen T.V. Dinners, as we know them today, were still somewhere in the future. But we had frozen dinners in the late 1920s. Not only were our lunches frozen from being kept in the freezing, cold cloakroom, but we usually consumed them in this frozen state. Frozen milk, eaten with a spoon from a pint Mason jar, made a pleasant change of texture from a frozen egg sandwich.

No effort was made to provide hot lunches until a soup kitchen was started around 1935. But because Mother had had a falling-out with the lady who was hired to do the cooking, we were not allowed to partake of the soup. Mother was stubborn in that way; if she made up her mind on some subject, no one could make her change. Sometimes we suffered because of her stubbornness, but we admired her for sticking to her guns.

KINDERGARTEN DAYS

In the fall of 1925, I started my education. I was not quite five years of age. Even though my two older sisters had been in school for two years, I had not absorbed much of their English. We spoke Finnish at home, and when I attempted to communicate with my Jewish teacher I encountered some difficulty. Thus it was, that when my teacher asked what my parents were doing, I replied, "They are piling riss." Martha was called upon to translate what I had tried to say: "They are piling brush." Isn't that what I said? A *risu* is a twig or a branch. Since Mother and Dad were clearing land, wasn't it natural to say they are piling "riss?" Really, I thought the teacher needed some lessons in Finnish. In spite of my rocky start in school, however, I learned quickly and managed to stay near the top of my class—not only in English, but in my other subjects as well.

On the whole, my kindergarten year passed uneventfully. Because of my tender years and small size, I was chosen to be the Baby Jesus in the annual Christmas program. I can still remember the nervousness I felt, fearing that I would spoil the program by

coughing or sneezing at the wrong time or—heaven forbid—
wetting myself. Fortunately, none of this happened, and the play
went off without incident.

Another vivid memory of that year was a cold January
afternoon spent sliding. Mother had made me a red woolen dress
with matching bloomers. Because we were the Beginners' class, or
kindergarten, we were dismissed an hour before the other classes.
So we spent the hour sliding down an icy bank until the horse-drawn
"bus" came to take us home.

On the long ride home I wondered why I felt a cold draft on my
backside. When I got home, Mother took one look at me, grabbed
me by the shoulder and forced me to bend over. Then, I really felt
a draft! While I had been sliding, I had worn-out not only my new
red bloomers, but my long-johns as well. My behind was bleeding
where the skin had rubbed off. Needless to say, Mother added a few
welts to the sore places I already had. The use of physical punishment was a common practice among many teachers and parents of
the time. Sparing the rod was almost unheard of by most parents.
Today's practice of grounding or taking away privileges would
have been meaningless to us considering we had no privileges, and
we were already grounded.

KAURA PUSSI-KAURA PUSSI

What is in a name? It depends on the name. Our name was
Kaurala which means "oat field" in the Finnish language. So the
big boys in school began to taunt us with *"Kaura Pussi-Kaura
Pussi"* which meant "Oat Bag-Oat Bag." Today, we can laugh
about it, but in those days, it was a cruel joke, one that caused us
many tears and somehow made us feel inferior.

There was one boy in particular who carried the joke farther
than mere name-calling. While we were at school he took our hats
and scarves in the dead of winter and threw them by the manure
heap. We were forced to go home bare-headed in the forty-below-
zero weather. It was several weeks later when his mother saw the
hats and scarves, and the items were returned to us. Years after-

ward, when he was in his late thirties, he apologized to Mother.

Then there were the times when one of the more popular girls convinced all the other girls to join with her in excluding the *Kaura Pussi* girls from their games. Many were the recess periods and lunch breaks when we stood alone, wishing desperately to be a part of the group, and almost hating our father for giving us the name Kaurala.

If Father had any clue as to how we felt, he never said anything; but he did remind us over and over that a name was only that—a name—and it was up to us to make that name mean something more than *Kaura Pussi.*

FINGERNAILS

I learned to put my fingers (and toes) into my mouth at a very tender age. By the time I was two or three, my fingers were in my mouth whenever I wasn't eating or talking. Every time I had my picture taken, I had both hands up to my mouth, chewing away at my fingernails. My nails were chewed to the quick, and even though they bled occasionally, that did not stop me from continuing the bad habit.

When I started kindergarten, however, I discovered my bad habit was causing my teacher some concern. I would not say she felt sorry for me, but she was concerned that I was leaving myself wide-open to infection every time I used the community paste jar or one of the modeling clays.

After countless warnings which fell on deaf ears, the teacher finally took drastic steps. She escorted me upstairs to the teacherage and liberally sprinkled my fingers with hot pepper. When I put my fingers to my mouth, I felt as though my mouth was on fire. The burning sensation was almost unbearable, and by the time I went home, my lips were blistered.

I did not receive any sympathy from Mother. She was one hundred percent in agreement with the teacher, and made it clear to me that it was about time something was done to break me of the disgusting habit. I never chewed my nails after that.

I began to take care of my hands and nails. My cuticles began to look normal, and my hang-nails gradually improved. By the time I was in my senior year of high school, I was the proud owner of extremely long fingernails.

On several occasions, Mother and Dad suggested I trim the nails to a more practical length. When these suggestions went unheeded for a few weeks, Dad took action. I was sitting at the kitchen table reading my history assignment, when Dad, seated in his usual place, said, "Miriam, let me see your hand." Not knowing what he had in mind, I absent-mindedly thrust out my right hand and kept on reading. Imagine my chagrin when I realized what he was up to! He had a pair of Mother's dressmaking shears, and was cutting my beautiful nails! He whacked off the nails on my right hand, then my left. The beautiful nails I had so lovingly nurtured were now merely ten clippings in an ashtray.

Years later, when I was trying to convince Dad to come to spend some time with me in Pennsylvania, I wrote and told him my nails needed trimming. Would you believe it? He came!

LESSONS LEARNED

It was in the winter of my first grade when I learned two of the most valuable lessons of all. The first of these was "do not repeat everything you hear." I had heard some of the big boys use a certain four-letter word, which, although I had no understanding of its meaning, I did know it was not an accepted word in the vocabulary of a six year old.

We were riding home on the bus one day when the incident occurred. The teachers had told Martha that they wanted her to deliver two quarts of milk the following day. One of the big boys picked up the conversation and changed it to "two farts of milk." Naturally, everyone on the bus laughed at that—and I, always ready for a good laugh, carried it a step farther and said, "Two f— ks of milk." Well, that brought about the desired laughter, so I repeated it a little louder this time, and again, the laughter followed.

But I had not counted on Martha's running home from the gate and telling Mother what I had said. By the time I reached the house, Mother was ready for me, switch in hand. I felt the switch on my bare bottom, and the resulting welts reminded me for several days of the not-to-be-repeated word. Even yet, at age 74, I cringe at the sound of the word. It has never been an accepted part of my vocabulary.

I remember quite well an incident that happened when my sister Esther was in the second grade, and I was in the first. Esther was always a well-behaved, quiet child who was quite timid around strangers and would often break into tears rather than speak in public. That year we had a teacher who had her favorites, and clearly Esther was not one of them. Neither was I, for that matter. This teacher seemed to enjoy making us feel inadequate. On this particular day, the assignment was for each student to go to the front of the room and recite a poem. When it was Esther's turn to recite, she broke into tears before she got to the front of the room. But she bravely swallowed her tears and recited: "Here I am, little Jumping Joan. When nobody's with me, I'm always alone."

The teacher criticized Esther's choice of a poem, as well as her delivery. How I suffered for Esther that day, because I knew just how she felt, and when we got home and Martha told Mother about it I felt worse.

Another lesson I learned that year concerned cheating. Our class assignment in spelling was a test on a group of words which the teacher had given us to study. I had carefully copied the words on a slip of paper, which I used when I practiced spelling them. When the test was over, and I had passed my paper to the front of the room according to procedure, I reached in my desk and took out the slip of paper to see if I had spelled the words correctly. One of the girls in the grade ahead of me saw me with the paper and marched up to the teacher, telling her I had cheated on the test.

The teacher did not ask for an explanation; she merely took my test paper from the pile on her desk and gave me a big, fat zero. That was punishment enough, but when I got home, I was punished again with the birch bough. Later on, when Mother was calmer, I was able to tell the truth of what happened. I learned a valuable lesson from this experience: never cheat! These lessons, painfully learned, have remained with me through all these years.

SWING BACK, UP ROUND UP ROUND UP

One of my favorite classes was Penmanship. The Palmer Method was the vogue in those years. How well I remember practicing my "push-pulls" and "circle-circles" to produce the perfect specimen to be sent to the district offices for grading. We made rows and rows of *See Me* "Swing back, up round up round up" and "over, over, over, up round up." The important thing was the wrist movement. Teacher could tell at a glance when a student was using a finger movement instead of the wrist. As a result, very few students went into the world with poor handwriting. Learning legible, readable handwriting was necessary in those days, and was an important part of the school's curriculum. We did not have computers and word processors like many of the students of today. In the years to come, the Palmer Method was scrapped, as were many other methods of teaching.

Self-expression is another facet of learning that was very evident in the schools of fifty or more years ago. We were graded on our ability to use words to describe a situation or a feeling. An emphasis was placed on correct grammar usage and accurate spelling, and we were often expected to recite poems and other pieces we had memorized. Memorization was an important part of our instruction.

In the area of mathematics, or as we called it, arithmetic, we were drilled from the second grade on in the times tables until we knew them by heart. We did not have computers and calculators like the students of today. We were expected to memorize our facts.

SCHOOL PICNICS

The last day of school was celebrated in many different ways. My first recollection of this occasion was the year I was in the first grade. The entire school population had a Free Day, and everyone was enjoying the beautiful early June morning. One of the big boys had brought his brand-new bicycle to school and was giving handle-bar rides to anyone who was brave enough to attempt it. When he asked Martha if she wanted a ride, she was more than willing to go. After all, she had never seen a bicycle this close, and besides, she was always ready to try the unknown. So she carefully climbed on and adjusted her skirt so it would not cause any embarrassment, and they were off!

Suddenly, the bicycle lurched and started to wobble on the loose gravel. Before we knew it, the bicycle was lying on its side in the road, and the two riders bit the dust. Martha did not hurt anything except her dignity, but her dress was torn, and her brand-new patent leather shoes were damaged beyond repair. Her dignity was hurt a second time when she got home. Mother gave Martha's behind a few whacks with the ruined patent leather slippers. It was one of the few times Martha was punished. It would be years before any of us got close to a bicycle again!

Another memorable Last Day of School was the year I was in fifth grade. The teachers had planned a picnic to be held on the school grounds. Each child was to bring an item of food for the occasion. When Mother saw the list of things we were to bring, she literally fumed. One of us was to bring a pound of franks; another, two cans of pork and beans; a third a dozen wiener buns; and a fourth, a jar of pickles. Why, that was almost a week's groceries! Ridiculous!

Mother decided we would take our own picnic lunch. To celebrate the occasion, she allowed Dad to buy some fancy cookies with pink, marshmallow-coconut covered tops. As we sat by ourselves at the picnic that day, eating our bologna sandwiches, I almost wished our mother was more like some of the other mothers. Even yet, many years later, when I see those marshmallow-type cookies, I can still recall that picnic.

In later years, the Last Day of School picnic came to mean outings at Birch Lake. But those never held the lasting memories that the earlier ones held for me.

THE CHRISTMAS PROGRAM

During our growing-up years, the biggest social event of the school year was the annual Christmas program. The entire student body was involved in the production; those who did not have a performing part took care of the stage props. Each year the parents provided the "stage curtains"—bedsheets which were pinned to a wire cable strung across the front of the classroom, thus separating the stage from the audience. Mother was always willing to donate a sheet for the occasion, and she usually picked out her best monogrammed, crochet-trimmed sheets. To her, this was the supreme sacrifice. The sheets our family used for everyday were made from four hundred-pound flour sacks sewn together.

The big boys were chosen to draw the curtains at the end of each number. Invariably, they were reluctant to take an active part in the performance, although they were willing to take part in the group singing. I remember one Christmas program in particular, when the entire student body was assembled on the stage to sing "Deck the Halls." The teacher, hiding in the corner off stage, had her pitch pipe ready to start the song. Suddenly, from one end of the group a lone voice sang "Deck" followed by another "Deck" coming from the opposite end. This went on for quite a few "Decks" until the audience broke out in gales of laughter. By this time everyone was laughing, and it was some time before the teacher regained her composure sufficiently to lead us in our song. I think this was one of our best programs, because the group laughter served to relax both the performers and the audience.

When I was in the third grade, I had to memorize *"The Story of the First Christmas."* It was a rather long recitation, but I went through it without a mistake. Another year, a group of us girls had a rather intricate dance number which we performed in crepe paper dresses, with tinsel garlands around our waists and tinsel "halos" on our heads. Crepe paper was the material of choice, as it was easy to work with and the cost was relatively small.

On the night of the program, families hurried through the evening milking and barn chores. Supper was very simple that night; most of us were too excited to eat, and I rather suspect parents were quite anxious as well. Sometimes, the school bus picked up the children a bit earlier so we would have time for some last-minute instructions or rehearsal. Otherwise, we would ride along with our parents and arrive at the school when it was almost show time. It was hard for Mother and Dad to find good seats; usually, the choice seats in the house were occupied by people who lived close to the school or those who had no children in school. They arrived early and took the front rows.

We usually had one long play on the program, with the remainder of the program consisting of poems, songs, and an occasional acrostic. For this number, nine or ten children, each carrying a large paper letter and reciting a line or two, spelled out the word "Christmas." The last child summarized the word with a slightly longer recitation. More often than not, a child came on stage carrying the letter upside down or mumbled his line before arriving in place. And if Christmas came out spelled "Christwas," with the "m" upside down, it was entirely proper— truly, "Christ was."

After the program there was a hush throughout the school as we waited for Santa Claus. He arrived, thumping through the back cloakroom with his bag of goodies. Every child received a small gift, even though it was only a popcorn ball wrapped in cellophane.

Usually, several weeks before Christmas, we drew names in school to assure every child of one gift. Some of the parents did not permit their children to participate in the name drawing, hence the reason for the popcorn balls. One year, when I was quite young, I drew a boy's name, and Mother made him a cotton shirt. I went to school and blabbed to everyone what my gift was going to be. Mother, for lack of anything else to use, wrapped the shirt in a yellow, Domino Cube-Sugar box. All gifts were wrapped in plain brown paper and tied with common store string. Fancy gift wrap was not popular until some years into the future. To us, any gift was something to be treasured no matter what the outside wrapping. The anticipation and eagerness with which we unwrapped our plain-wrapped gifts brought us as much—if not more—pleasure than many of the fancy, foil-wrapped gifts of today.

After Santa had emptied his pack, we reluctantly prepared to leave for home. All the way home we bubbled over our gifts and the general success of the program. The memories remained with us for weeks and helped us through the cold, dark days of January.

THE LUNCH BOXES

When I was about ten years old, I was responsible for packing the lunches for all of us. Martha was still at home, but Mother did not want to put too much pressure on her, so I was elected for the task. In those days, everyone carried their lunch in a five-pound *Swifts Silverleaf Lard* pail with a pint-size screw-cap Mason jar for the milk.

Packing four lunches each morning took time and a lot of imagination, especially when I had one egg to use for four sandwiches. So I beat the egg with a fork, added a little milk, and spread the mixture ever so thin in a skillet, to make a large circle. Cut into quarters, this provided a piece of egg big enough to make a sandwich. Occasionally, we had leftover pork or venison roast, but most of the time it was jelly or marmalade sandwiches. One year, Dad brought a jar of peanut butter home from the neighborhood store. I made peanut butter sandwiches for everyone, but they were returned that night. The peanut butter stuck to the roof of the mouth and the teeth. We never had peanut butter sandwiches after that.

Another time, Dad brought home a box of *Nabisco Shredded-Wheat Biscuits*. I guess the only part of the label he understood was the word "biscuit." I put one in each lunch pail. Can you imagine us as we tried to eat a dry, crumbly shredded-wheat biscuit?

We usually had homemade cake or cookies in our lunch pails. Pie was never part of our lunch, because plastic pie carriers had not been discovered yet and plastic wrap had not yet become a landfill problem. (Neither had aluminum foil for that matter, yet we somehow survived without it.) However, in some respects, our lunches were superior to those some of our friends carried. At least, we had real butter on our bread; some of the others had pork fat on theirs. Some of our friends carried stacks of cold pancakes or

French toast in their lunch pails.

Once in a while we had an apple or half an orange as a special treat. When my brother Lauri entered first grade, he had a whole orange in his lunch pail. Because it was such a treat to him, he could not quite bring himself to eat it. So he played with it until the bell rang signifying the end of the lunch period. The teacher, who certainly should have shown more understanding, snatched the orange out of Lauri's hands and tossed it in the wastebasket. From that day forward, Lauri's enthusiasm for school dropped to zero.

EIGHTH-GRADE GRADUATION

Prior to World War II, graduation from eighth grade was a big step in a student's life. But before we could graduate, we had to pass state board examinations in all of our subjects. These examinations were held toward the end of the school year, and the results would not be known until a few days before graduation.

When Esther's class graduated, it was the smallest group to graduate, so their ceremony was combined with several other schools in the area. Although I was not able to attend her graduation—due to the location and limited space, attendance was for parents only—I can still remember what she wore. She had a peach-colored organdy dress with rows of ruffles on each side and a wide sash tied in the back. On her feet she wore the tiniest tan pumps with a Cuban heel.

The following year, 1933, was my turn to graduate from eighth grade. There were fifteen boys and seven girls in my group. Two of the girls had come from the nearby town of Babbitt, where the entire school population was around ten students. I remember I wrote and read the Class Poem, in which I briefly described each student. Our speaker was Reverend Tamminen from Ely. He spoke of the fast-changing times and of our need to be able to accept and adapt.

Several of my male classmates were called into the service during World War II; some were killed in action and others were injured. One of my classmates was taken prisoner by the Japanese and was never heard from after that.

Graduation from the eighth grade ended the education process for many children in those days. Since so much of the area was farmland, the boys were needed at home to help with the farm work. And with an eighth-grade diploma in hand, it was relatively easy to find employment away from the farm.

HIGH SCHOOL

Until the middle 1930s, only two years of high school were provided at the local level. Juniors and seniors had to leave home to complete their high school education. In 1934, Esther as a fifteen year old was quite naive, and being the first to complete the two years at the local high school, had to come to terms with breaking the family ties. She enrolled at Ely Memorial High School. I can only imagine what she must have experienced in those first few days—alone, among strangers, being forced from a class of four to a class of a hundred or more; not knowing her way around town, much less, not knowing her way around school. It is a wonder she was able to cope. But cope she did, and after the first grading period, when she received a "D" in public speaking, she attained the honor roll each month, thus proving she was no dumb country cousin.

The following year, when the local High School was closed, Ora and I joined Esther and attended Ely Memorial High. The three of us shared a room—and a bed—in a home in Ely. I would say a friend's home, but, to be honest, we had never met the couple before. It was a totally spontaneous, spur-of-the-moment decision on the part of Mother and Dad.

We settled in on Labor Day, and the following day Esther took us to school and helped us get registered for our classes. It was quite an experience for us, having a choice in what courses to take. The first few days were traumatic. We had to learn our way around the school, make new friends, and, in general, adjust to the new routine. But we survived and by the time the school year ended, we knew most of our classmates, if not by name, at least, by face and classroom number.

Weekends were the best part of the year. Every Friday afternoon, Dad came to take us home. On Saturday, we washed and ironed our clothes, shampooed our hair, and took a good hot sauna bath. Our home away from home had no bathing facilities—not even a lavatory sink for brushing the teeth or washing the face. However, there was a toilet in a small closet in a remote corner of the basement. In order to find our way to the john, it was necessary to turn on the light at the head of the stairs. On more than one occasion the light was suddenly snapped off, leaving the occupant of the throne in the dark. The older daughter of the house took it upon herself to conserve electricity in this way.

The Babbitt school district helped to defray the cost of our education to the tune of ten dollars a month for each of us. Dad faithfully turned this over to the host family. Besides the monetary compensation, each week he and Mother provided several quarts of milk, cream, butter, potatoes and other produce to make sure we did not go hungry. And when the hog was slaughtered in the fall, most of the choice cuts went to "keeping the girls fed."

Our social life in Ely was practically non-existent. We had no close friends and no invitations to go anywhere. Slumber parties had not as yet come into vogue, although the three of us sleeping in one bed provided our own slumber party five nights a week. About once a month we did manage to attend a movie at the local theater. Because adult admissions cost considerably more than children's tickets, we persuaded Ora to purchase the tickets for us. She was so small, she easily passed for a twelve year old. This went on until one day the ticket taker refused to let us in with a child's ticket. Needless to say, we could not afford too many movies after that.

During our high school years Esther and I had summer jobs. When Esther was seventeen and I was going on sixteen, we had worked in Babbitt. I went to work for Mrs. DuCharme, who had recently given birth to her first child. Esther went to work for Mrs. Emanuelson, who had two children, Jimmy and Bobby. Everyday I had to wash diapers by hand in the bathtub, rinse them three times, and hang them out to dry. This was 1936 B.D.— Before Disposables. Esther's job was a little easier; at least her two boys were house broken.

The following summer, Esther went to work at Lenont's farm, which was located where the town of Babbitt is today. Lenont's was a large operation at the time, and provided jobs for most of the young men of the area. Mother and I were quite apprehensive about Esther going there; we were sure it was more than she could handle. However, Esther surprised us and remained there almost two years.

When I graduated from Embarrass High School in 1937, I went to work at Lenont's alongside Esther. We took care of the cooking and serving of meals to the farmhands. Every morning we were up before dawn, and by 5:30 we had breakfast ready for the hungry men. Breakfast consisted of fried potatoes, eggs, side pork or bacon, biscuits or toast, and gallons of boiled coffee. There were at least a dozen men to feed every morning, noon, and night, six days a week.

While working on Lenont's farm during the late 1930s, I observed some unusual ways of preserving food. Mrs. Walker, who headed the kitchen operation, had her own unique ways of preserving food. Eggs were put into a water-glass solution which kept them fresh for months. Water-glass is a substance composed of sodium silicate, potassium silicate, or both. It was dissolved in hot water, and was used quite often for preserving eggs, to insure a constant supply during the hens' off-season.

Another strange method of food preservation was Mrs. Walker's way with pork chops. In the fall, when the hogs were butchered, the pork loins were cut into chops, which were then pan-fried until almost done. They were layered into large barrels with rendered pork fat poured between the layers. Stored in a cool place, the chops prepared this way remained wholesome until spring. I can still picture Esther and me, groping through the pork fat, trying to get enough pork chops to feed the men for supper. Oh, for the happy days of the past, when life was simple and filled with imagination!

Esther graduated from Ely Memorial High in the spring of 1936. The following September, Ora and I transferred to the new Embarrass High School which had been constructed the previous year. Although my class was the second to graduate from the new school, we were the first class to have attended our senior year there. The Embarrass High School was remodeled and enlarged in the years after World War II. Due to decreasing enrollment, however, it was closed in 1970. Gone were the days of the one- or two-room schoolhouse.

PASTIMES ON THE FARM

"Some of the neighbors had
gasoline-powered washing machines;
how we envied them..."

FUN AND GAMES

Living on the farm as we did had its limitations as well as its advantages. The nearest neighbors were more that a mile away, so we learned to entertain ourselves by creating our own games and fun. One of Dad's first priorities was to build a playhouse for his girls. It was the envy of all who saw it, and we spent more than one summer in it playing house, paper dolls, school, and other games. We would hurry through our chores in the morning, then go to spend the rest of the day in the playhouse. It was great because we could make as much mess as we liked; when the clutter got too bad, we "cleaned house" by scrubbing the floor, rearranging the furniture, and washing the windows. We had two real windows, which, even though they did not open, did provide plenty of daylight.

Esther was always the realist when it came to our games and playtime. One summer, when Esther was about ten, we each had created our own little playhouse. Esther built her house on the top of the pigs' shelter. Not content to merely play at cooking, she built a real fire in a tin-can-and-stone arrangement which she called her cookstove. Fortunately for the pigs and the rest of us, the fire was kept under control; Mother knew nothing of this until some years later.

Another summer we were busy making furniture for the tiny rag dolls we had created out of some of Mother's carpet rags. The dolls were less than six inches tall, so the furniture had to be quite tiny. Esther used several *Prince Albert Tobacco* cans to build a table and chairs– a bed, and other furnishings for her dolls. Her prize creation was a tiny tricycle with handlebars that worked and tiny pedals that actually made the front wheel turn. We did not have Erector Sets or Lincoln Logs, or any of the wonderful building sets of today. We built our own out of materials at hand, using whatever tools we could lay our hands on. When my brother Paul was given a set of Tinker Toys for Christmas one year, we felt very rich to have a chance to work with real store-bought building materials.

We were lucky in that a friend of Mother's worked at the public library in Ely. Whenever there were books to be discarded, this friend remembered us. We would receive a whole box full of books in time for summer vacation. How we enjoyed those books! We read them over and over, until they literally fell apart. There

Miriam, Esther, Martha and Ora Kaurala outside their playhouse, Babbitt, Minn. 1924.

were books of fairy tales and princesses, stories of Ab the Cave-man, the sabre-toothed tigers, and the extinct woolly mammoth.

On the few occasions when neighbor children came to visit, we would play "Lead and Tin," "Spin the Bottle," or "I Met a Little Girl with a Basket." When we played "I Met a Little Girl With a Basket," Esther would usually stump everyone with her strange basket fillers. For example, who would ever guess that "something that begins with 'R' and 'P' " could mean ric-rac and piping or that "C.G." would mean coffee grounds!

Sometimes we played store in the kitchen pantry. It was very suitable for this purpose, with its shelves for merchandise, and a door that could be propped open during "business hours." When the local storekeeper in town was robbed at gunpoint, we recreated the incident for months afterward. We had heard this noteworthy robbery news in school. In our small community, where such things seldom happened, this was big news. As the story made its rounds, it was magnified and embroidered over and over. The truth of it was that no one was hurt. The gun misfired and only a small amount of money was involved.

Our game version of the robbery was not true-to-life. One of us was the storekeeper who was asleep in the corner of the pantry. The would-be robber forced his way into our store, making enough racket to arouse the storekeeper, who rubbed his eyes and in a trembling voice asked, *"Kuka se?"* (Who is it?) The robber would point his weapon and answer, *"Anna rahat."* (Give me your money.) Mr. Storekeeper reluctantly opened the cash register and gave part of the money to the robber, but the robber was not satisfied. He raised the gun a little higher and said, *"Anna Kaiklci!"* (Give all of it!) It was then that the robber tried to fire the gun. Fortunately, it failed to fire, giving the storekeeper a chance to get away. The unhappy robber dropped his gun and money and fled on foot. Not a very exciting game, to be sure, but to us it was great fun—especially when some of the neighbor's children joined in the game.

In the summer, when the evenings were long and lazy, we spent hours chasing and catching fireflies. We put them into a glass jar to make a flashlight, or we rubbed their bellies around a finger to create a ring that glowed in the dark.

Winter evenings brought their own special fun. Dad made us a heavy wooden sled which we used for years. It was big enough for three or four to ride at one time. We spent many a moonlit winter evening sledding down the hill into the cow pasture. (In later years, Brother Paul constructed a toboggan slide on this same hill, providing fun for the next generation of the family.) Sometimes, when Mother and Dad were all caught up with their chores, they bundled us up, and with old Jerry pulling the sleigh, took us to visit the neighbors.

Another favorite game of ours was a bit like "Blind Man's Buff." Only, instead of having a whole group play, one of us was blindfolded, and another led her around. We were not allowed to speak except to say "step up" or "step down." I will never forget the time Esther was leading me, and she said, "Step down," and I went crashing into a deep gravel pit! I suffered a bad cut on my arm, but I was afraid to tell Mother. She would have been angry with us. So I nursed the cut the best I could, and in time, the gravel worked its way out. For years afterward, I had a bad scar.

When Mother and Dad had their night school citizenship classes, we were anxious to have them go off and leave us alone. We were never afraid to be left without a baby sitter. By the time Martha was ten, she was a perfectly trustworthy, capable baby sitter. We played "Lead and Tin" or "I Met a Little Girl With a Basket" or "Old Maid" until it was time for bed. Occasionally, a card game would end in a minor hassle. Nobody liked to be the Old Maid. But on the whole, we enjoyed those evenings by ourselves.

One can well imagine that these evenings out meant more to Mother than they did to us. After all, she was totally tied down to her family and the farm chores. Besides, she was eager to learn and make the most of her opportunity for education. As part of her citizenship training, she had to memorize the names and dates of all our presidents, as well as the names of the president's cabinet members. Our education was never as complete!

Another memory I have concerning Mother's night school

days involves our various attempts at cooking. Once, we tried to make ice cream in Mother's shiny, tin-plated freezer. It was in the winter, so ice was no problem. We had watched Mother prepare the cream mixture, so we were confident we knew the procedure. However, something went wrong in our operation, and the end result was not ice cream, but lumps of sweet, vanilla-flavored butter. That ended our ice cream making, at least for the time being.

On several other occasions while Mother was attending night school, we entertained ourselves by making candy. As I think back on it now, I shudder at the risks we were taking; we were placing ourselves in jeopardy, as well as risking the chance of burning the house down. We put plain granulated sugar into a tin cup, removed the lamp chimney and then held the cup over the kerosene lamp, until the sugar caramelized. Then we poured the hot syrup into a bowl full of snow, to cool it quickly. This was a very easy way to make candy, but it was also very dangerous.

Once, we even tried to make peanut butter. It was shortly after Christmas, and Santa had been overly generous with peanuts. So we sat and shelled peanuts until we had enough. Then Martha set up Mother's meat grinder, and we took turns grinding the elusive kernels. For some reason, they kept rolling around in the grinder, and we had to push them into the coil of the worm. We finally completed the grinding process; then we decided something else was needed to make a true peanut butter. So we mixed the peanut puree with some of Mother's home-churned butter. I wondered why it did not taste right, it definitely was not *Jiffy* peanut butter!

WITH A SONG IN MY HEART

From the time Martha entered kindergarten, songs were very much a part of our life. There were songs for every occasion, for every season of the year, for every holiday, for the start of classes each morning, and the closing of the school day. We sang "Good Morning Dear Teacher" each morning and "Let Us Put Our Books Away" before we were dismissed. On Halloween, we sang "Here We Come, Here We Come, Jack-o'-Lanterns All." On Thanksgiving day it was "Thanksgiving Day is Coming, So Mister Turkey Said," or "Over the River and Through Woods." We had several songs for Christmas, such as, "Down the Chimney, Broad and Black, Comes Old Santa Claus," "Oh, Santa Claus is Coming and the Stockings in a Row," or "Jolly Old St. Nicholas." In February, we honored Washington and Lincoln on their birthdays, and on Valentine's Day we sang "Mr. Postman, Have You Any Valentines?" When March winds blew and spring was in the air, we sang "When Spring Rises, Out Through the Woods," and following that we sang songs to "Lady April, Lady April." When it was May, we greeted her with "Off to the Woods on a Bright May Morning, Gathering Flowers for a Holiday." And, of course, there were songs for Mother's Day, "M is for the Million Things She Gave Me" and "Cross My Heart, Mother, I Love You." Before we began our summer vacation, we sang "What Shall We Do On Our Holiday?"

During our play periods in school, we sang and danced to songs like "How'dy Do, My Partner, How'dy Do Today?" or "Thief, Yes, Thief, That is Your Name, For You Stole My Little Friend." To be sure there was "A Tisket, A Tasket," "Here We Dance Looby-Loo," "Oh, Have You Seen the Muffin Man?" and the good old favorite, "London Bridge." There were songs about people, like "Bobby Shaftoe's Gone to Sea," and "Oh Where Have You Been, Billy Boy?" We sang about girls like "Mary Had a Little Lamb" or "Have You Seen Polly's Bonnet?" Yes, we had songs in our hearts, every day of the school year.

We raised our voices in song about other things, such as, "Up was I on My Grandpa's Farm on a May Morning Early" and "Susie, Little Susie, What Stirs in the Hay?" We had several songs about birds, "Oh, I am Robin Red Breast" and "Pretty Little Bluebirds, Why Do You Fly?" We sang about "The Friendly Cow All Red and White," "Once there Lived a Little Man, Where a Little River Ran," and "Click, Clack, Clack, Hear How the Shoes are Dancing." The list could go on and on, but suffice it to say everything inspired a song or two, and in spite of the harsh times and a lack of material things, we always had a song in the heart.

PLAYING MAYTAG WASHER

Doing the laundry for a family of nine was quite a task, especially in the winter months. Mother usually performed this duty in the dressing room of the sauna, where she had an old wood-burning, potbellied stove, the old wringer-wash-tub stand, and her faithful copper-bottomed boiler.

When Dad was home, he would carry water to fill the boiler and start the fire in the stove. After the barn chores were done, Mother gathered up all the soiled clothes she could find and carried them to the sauna. Then she sorted them into several piles, according to soil, and started the task of washing them. She took hot water from the boiler and mixed it with some of the cold water to make the wash water.

With her scrub board and bar of *Fels Naptha Soap,* she proceeded to wash each item of laundry. Then they were ready for the dip in the boiler. Every piece of washing went through this step; the delicate fabrics got merely a quick dip, while other fabrics had a longer stay in the sanitizing hot water. After the boil she fished the items from the boiler with a long, wooden stick, and then put them into the first cold rinse. This was followed by a swishing in the water, and then, through the wringer into the final rinse. A little bluing was used in the final rinse—equivalent to the fabric softeners we use today. Then came the hard part—drying the clothes. Winter or summer, Mother always hung her washing outdoors. In the winter, the clothes froze before she got them on the lines.

It was a sight to see, especially in mid-winter, when nine or more pairs of long underwear were hanging from the line with the drop-seats on five of them frozen in the open position. Of course, the clothes did not dry completely, but Mother loved the fresh outdoor smell of her clean laundry. After they were thoroughly frozen, she carried them in, a few at a time, to finish drying in the house. The heavy denim overalls and throw rugs were hung in the sauna to dry overnight.

In the summer months, the laundry was our job. We made a

game of it and called it "Playing Maytag Washer." During these summer months we washed the clothes out doors by the big white birch tree near the sauna. It was a bit harder, carrying the clumsy wringer-stand and tubs outside, but we did not mind the extra work. After all, we were not planning to go anywhere when the laundry was done.

Some of the neighbors had gasoline powered washing machines; how we envied them, as we had to do the washing the hard way. We had never seen a washing machine, much less, seen one in operation, but our imaginations helped to make this chore a pleasant one. So we played "Maytag" until the washing was done.

Before we took over the entire laundry operation in the summer months, we started out with "small steps" to help Mother with the task. Each of us was assigned a special job to do. My first introduction to the washing procedure was the handkerchiefs. This was in the days before tissue was introduced. Picture, if you will, the number of handkerchiefs used by a family of nine as the whole family suffered through a summer cold. More than once I gagged as I tried to scrub the thick, yellow slime from the hankies.

Then there were the diapers. I was not quite eight when my sister Elsie was born in 1927. She was my responsibility. I learned to change diapers, to bathe and dress her, and to amuse her whenever I was not at school. Mother used a diaper pail for the wet and soiled diapers and, invariably, it was my job to wash them. Mother often teased me in later years about how squeamish I was washing the diapers. I used a stick to swish the diapers in the water, trying to remove the nauseating chunks before I could bring myself to actually touch them. This, too, I found was a vital part of my home economics training for the future.

I took care of Elsie the entire summer of my ninth year. Mother had promised me a reward at the end of the summer. My reward was a boy doll named Eric. He cost all of 98 cents in the Sears Roebuck catalog. He was a beautiful doll, dressed in a blue-and-pink print romper, and he even had black patent leather shoes and white socks. How I treasured him! For several years Eric sat in the place of honor—on top of the piano. One day, while I was at school, Elsie managed to climb to the top of the piano and took Eric. He was never the same after that. Even though Mother washed and ironed his clothes, his chipped nose and chewed-up fingers were a constant reminder of his ordeal. Poor Eric, from that day on one of his blue eyes always looked downward.

When my brother Lauri was born in 1929, he became Esther's responsibility for the summer. Even after the school year started, she dressed him every morning. When he demanded he have high boots and breeches like his older brother Paul, she had to struggle with him every day before she got herself ready for school.

Mother continued to do her washing the hard way until about 1940, when Esther acquired a used gasoline-operated machine. Esther had been employed at Montgomery Ward's Mail Order establishment at the time. One of her co-workers was advertising a used gasoline-powered washing machine for sale. Esther purchased the machine for around fifteen dollars. Mother used the machine for about twelve years until rural electrification arrived, then she was able to purchase an electrically-operated machine. However, she refused to see the merits of a clothes dryer until she was in her seventies. She had once observed a neighbor lady pulling a mass of tangled sheets out of a dryer and decided she did not want her sheets coming out in a hopeless tangle. But after my brother Paul bought her a heavy-duty Maytag dryer, she often wished she had seen the wisdom of it years before.

THE BOUDOIR DOLL

In the late 1920s, one of the most popular fads among girls of all ages was the Boudoir Doll. I like to think of her as the Barbie Doll of that era. Boudoir Dolls were homemade—a rag doll of ridiculous proportions. Her arms and legs were long and thin, made to be tied to a doorknob or bed post, or, occasionally, arranged on the bed pillows. She wore silk pajamas, preferably of black satin, with contrasting trim of white lace and narrow satin ribbon.

Martha had spent a few days in Ely, visiting some of her preteen friends. It was there she became acquainted with the

Boudoir Doll. She studied it carefully, committing each detail to memory, knowing she could easily duplicate it at home to make a Boudoir Doll of her own.

So when Martha came home, she managed to con Mother into giving her a clean unbleached muslin flour sack which she used to make the body of the doll. I remember watching her as she used the old treadle machine to sew the parts together. Then she turned them right-side-out and stuffed them carefully with small pieces of rags. Esther and I wanted to help with this part of the project, but Martha knew exactly how much stuffing was needed: too much, and the limbs could not be tied into knots; too little, and the doll would not be able to hold up her head. The doll's face was embroidered after the stuffing was completed. Martha had precisely the right ideas of how to create the "come hither" look in the doll's eyes and the half-smiling mouth. The result was truly amazing. How I envied Martha's creativity!

The doll needed hair, and because Martha wanted it to be a true work of art, she used all her powers of persuasion on Mother. Martha knew Mother had a secret hidden in a dresser drawer—a dark brown hairpiece Mother had worn years ago, when huge hats were the height of fashion. With the huge hats, women wore large hairdos, and because Mother was not blessed with a luxurious head of hair, she needed the extra piece to fill in the large size of the hat.

Since becoming a farm wife and mother, she had no use for hairpieces and over-sized hats. Graciously, she donated the treasured human hair to the bald-but-beautiful Boudoir Doll. In no time at all, Martha had sewn the hair in place and had arranged an upswept hairdo held securely with a Heinz pickle pin. (As a promotional gimmick, the Heinz Company would send a pickle pin to anyone requesting one.)

For the doll's outfit, Martha took the black satin lining out of an old coat and created the satin pajamas. Lace for the trimming was a bit harder to find, but she managed to salvage a few inches from the collar of an old dress in Mother's rag box. The picot-edged ribbon for Boudoir Doll's sash came from the ties of a baby's sacque.

When the doll was completed, it was quite a creation, and Martha was very proud of her accomplishment. Truly, it was beautiful, and added a nice accent note to the bedroom, whether hanging from the doorknob, or sitting demurely on the bed with knees folded under her arms.

But alas, Martha's Boudoir Doll's days were numbered, and she came to a very unexpected end. One day, not much more than a week into her life, Brother Paul saw the doll hanging from the bed post. Naturally, Brother Paul was curious about the doll and wanted to get a closer look. Before Martha knew what was happening, Paul had the doll and was running with it, with Martha close behind. A fight ensued, but Martha was clearly the winner, while Paul, the loser, was crying as loud as any four year old who had fought a battle and lost.

Mother, in her usual wisdom, did the only thing possible in a situation like this: she snatched the doll and without words, threw it into the kitchen cook stove, where a hot fire was burning. I remember watching as Mother closed the stove lid, and I saw the flames consume the satin pajamas, the upswept hairdo, and, finally, the half-smiling mouth.

Was that the end of the Boudoir Doll? Not quite. When I emptied the ashes on the following Saturday, I found the charred and blackened remains of the pickle pin.

MILKING THE COWS

When Esther and I were thirteen and eleven years old respectively, Mother decided it was time we learned to milk a cow. To prepare ourselves for this task, we put on long-sleeved shirts and tied kerchiefs over our hair to make sure no hairs would get into the milk. Then we washed our hands thoroughly after which we took a basin of warm water and a soft cloth to scrub the udder and nipples of the cows we had been assigned to milk.

Esther was the designated milker of Moolie, and I of Mansu. We each took a milking stool and positioned ourselves in the proper place for milking. Mother showed us how to lean our foreheads on the cow's belly, just above the "faucets." Then, when we were nicely settled, she gave us each a pail to fill.

After several fruitless pulls, I finally managed to squirt a thin stream of milk, which, for some reason, missed the pail and found its way down the long sleeves of my shirt. A few more pulls, and I managed to coax another trickle of milk. This time it wet my knees and upper legs. On the next attempt, I thought I was getting the hang of it when I finally managed to squirt the stream into the pail.

About this time, Mansu was getting impatient; she had never felt fingers like mine before. She turned her head to see what was going on, and just then she swished her tail to chase a fly, momentarily blinding me. I dropped the milk pail. In my haste to get up, I knocked down the stool, which then hit Mansu in the leg. She, in turn, kicked the over-turned milk pail. The resulting clatter was enough to excite Moolie, who thus far had been cooperating with Esther. Needless to say, Moolie's cooperation ended right there, and Esther's attempt at milking turned out to be as fruitless as mine.

Mother failed to see the humor of the situation. She blamed us for the entire series of events. As she cleaned up the mess and finished milking the cows, she muttered to herself, *"Sano paska ja tee ite."* (Say shit, and do it yourself.) She never asked us to help with milking after that.

THE SHINGLE MILL

I will never forget the summer when the whole family was involved in making cedar shingles. Dad had acquired a gas-powered saw mill which would shave off one-quarter-inch thick slices from cedar logs. The logs were cut to about fourteen-inch lengths and were soaked in a creosote solution before the shingles were made. One of us girls had the job of fishing the logs out of the creosote tubs while another girl put fresh logs in to soak.

Dad had the responsibility of the machine itself. He kept the motor running and guided the logs as the shingles were shaved off. Here, the third girl had the task of receiving the shingles and stacking them in neat piles.

From breakfast until lunch and from lunch until supper, we were kept busy at the shingle mill. Before the season was over, there were stacks of shingles in every conceivable place. The following summer, Dad put new shingle roofs on the sauna, the woodshed, the garage, the hayloft and the playhouse. The barn? No, the barn had a galvanized roof, and did not require shingles.

TEN-GOING-ON-TWENTY

To most parents in the 1920s and 1930s, a child's tenth birthday was a major milestone to be celebrated in a special way. When a child reached the age of ten, he was then said to be "going on twenty;" at the age twenty, he would be "going on thirty" for the next ten years.

When Martha celebrated her tenth birthday, she received many special gifts. The best of these was a real Waterman fountain pen with a gold-colored point and a black silk ribbon that could be worn around her neck. Her other special gifts included a pair of long silk stockings, and a pair of real store-bought silk panties. How I envied her and wished my tenth birthday would hurry so I, too, could have silk stockings and underwear.

But by the time I reached that milestone, the Great Depression was on its way, so the silk stockings and fountain pen were not among my gifts. However, I did receive a pair of peach-colored rayon panties which faded to an ugly, muddy ecru after the first washing. The first rayon fabrics were quite unstable~ not only as to colors, but to laundering in general.

More important than the panties, I received a live Leghorn chicken for my birthday. Mother and Dad had arranged to purchase some laying hens from a friend in White Iron, and when the lady found out it was my birthday, she generously threw in an extra hen for me. For a few days after I was very happy, secure in the knowledge that I was the sole owner of a living, breathing, egg-laying hen.

However, when I came home from school about a week later,

I was devastated to learn that my little white hen had expired. She was probably sick when I acquired her—no one ever knew for sure. I was broken-hearted over my loss. I stood in the chimney corner in the living room, crying my eyes out. After what seemed like hours, I thought I heard someone telling me: "Miriam, you are a big girl now. You are 'ten-going-on-twenty' and you should not be crying over a chicken." Whether I actually heard this or not, I made up my mind, then and there, to dry my tears and start acting like a ten year old. From that day on, whenever I had a disappointment or sad situation to face, I thought of my tenth birthday, and I remembered not to cry over a chicken.

THE GREAT DEPRESSION YEARS

"He wore no gloves nor overshoes, and his teeth
chattered as he held his cold hands to the
warmth of the kitchen stove..."

HOME HEALTH CARE

During the Depression years and the dark years of World War II, health care was largely a matter of home remedies, with the help of patent medicines such as were available through the Watkins man or the local general store. *Watkins Liniment* was used not only for human ailments, but for farm animals as well. Babies cried for *Castoria Syrup,* and women used *Lydia Pinkham's* for feminine discomfort. P.M.S. was unheard of and menopause was tolerated as a welcome end to the fear of pregnancy. Frequently birth control was achieved through the use of self-control, hence, the large families!

Preventive medicine in our family consisted of using unslaked lime water to rinse our mouth after using the family toothbrush. By the time I was eight or nine, Dad started us on Cod-Liver Oil. Even yet, I shudder as I think about swallowing a spoonful of that oily, fishy, foul-tasting stuff. Every day, Dad lined us up and gave us our daily dose. Mother tried to keep a special spoon for this ceremony, but invariably, she managed to pick up that spoon to stir her coffee. There was something about the cod-liver oil—the odor and greasiness remained on the spoon even after washing it in hot water and *Fels Naptha Soap.*

For a toothache, Dad soaked a piece of cotton with camphorated oil which we placed on the offending tooth. The same remedy was used for an earache. When we had a cold, Mother warmed a piece of flannel and, after smearing our chest with camphorated oil, wrapped our chest in the warm flannel. Later, when the financial picture was a little better, we had *Vicks Vaporub* or *Mentholatum* for a chest rub.

Until the time I reached my teens, I suffered from frequent headaches. I was never examined by a physician, so we did not know the cause. How well I remember staying home from school for a day or two while the headache ran its course. Mother would put a cool, wet washcloth on my forehead. This gave temporary relief until the washcloth picked up the heat from my feverish head. Occasionally, if the headache pain was too intense, Mother gave me a *Bayer Aspirin* to relieve the pain.

Emergencies were few and far between. I went to the emergency room only once. When I was fifteen years old, Esther and I were racing to the door, and I sprained my wrist. Because it swelled so fast and turned a deep purple, Dad decided to take me to the Ely Hospital. As it turned out, the wrist was not broken, but the sprain required several weeks of rest and recuperation. That same year, I went to the emergency room with Paul when he suffered a bad cut on his hand. I will never forget the feeling I had as I watched the doctor suture the hand. Brother Paul had chopped right through his hand, close to the thumb. Fortunately, he missed the bone when he swung the axe, so, aside from the temporary inconvenience, he suffered no permanent damage.

On another occasion, I accompanied Dad when he took my sister Elsie to the emergency room. Elsie had a huge boil in her armpit. The boil was lanced, and a drainage tube was inserted to promote healing. For weeks afterward, Elsie had to remain at home until the infection subsided. This was the extent of my acquaintance with doctors and hospitals until I went to the university to study.

Our dental care was provided through the public school system. The county office sent a dentist to the school every year or two. He made a preliminary visit a week or so before his scheduled work session, and notices were sent to the parents, informing them of what work was to be done. Usually, extraction of the tooth was necessary. The going rate was twenty-five cents for an extraction, which had to be paid in advance. One year, I was scheduled to have one of my baby molars extracted. Dad paid for this, along with whatever work my sisters were to have done. However, my baby tooth conveniently fell out a few days before the dentist's arrival, and I was given a refund of twenty-five cents. I believe that was the first time in my life I had ever had a whole quarter, so I went to the store and bought two *Baby Ruth* candy bars—one for me and one for my girlfriend. When I got home, Mother was ready for me. I had forgotten how quickly Martha could run home from the school bus! Lucky for me, I still had the fifteen cents change to give Mother. It would be quite some time before I purchased another candy bar.

Living as we did, in the uncivilized wilderness, we were prone to insect bites and bee stings, especially on our frequent berry-picking excursions. When we were attacked by a hornet or wasp, the best available treatment was wet mud. If this was applied immediately after the attack, there was little swelling or discomfort. One time, however, I was stung in the middle of my forehead, and in my haste to get away from the angry hornets, I forgot about the wet mud. By the time I reached home and safety, my eyes were swollen, and the sting was causing considerable discomfort. Mother did what she could to ease the pain, but the swelling continued until I could barely see. The next day, a peddler and his wife happened to come to the house. The woman smeared some foul-smelling brown liquid on my forehead and eyelids. Whatever it was, it reduced the swelling overnight, and by the following afternoon I was as good as new.

Mother usually treated our mosquito bites with her old stand-by, camphorated oil. It was also her remedy for a stuffy nose and countless other ills. For internal use, such as mild stomach upsets, Dad gave us a few drops of turpentine on a lump of sugar. The turpentine was a special *Spirits of Turpentine* and was safe to eat. If we had eye problems, such as dry, itchy eyes, Dad sprinkled a few grains of salt into the eyes. Years later, when I mentioned this to my optometrist, he said that this was a way of helping Nature; dry, itchy eyes are Nature's way of showing us there are not enough tears to bathe the eyes. And what are tears, but salt water? Yes, our home health care may have been crude, but it served the purpose—and we grew up in spite of it.

THE COLD AND CHILLY MAN

During the difficult years of the Depression, it was not unusual to have a stranger appear at the door. Most of them were itinerant peddlers trying to sell pots and pans, yard goods, or medications, such as *Rose Salve*. No matter what the time of day or day of the week, Mother always invited the stranger in for a cup or coffee, or, if it was near mealtime, she invited him to share the meal with us.

One stranger left a lasting impression on us. He arrived late at night on one of the coldest nights of the winter. He was almost frozen when he arrived, and when he stepped into the kitchen we were fascinated by the long icicles hanging from his nose and his handlebar mustache. He wore no gloves nor overshoes, and his teeth chattered as he held his cold hands to the warmth of the kitchen stove and said, "Gee, but it's cold and chilly out tonight."

He had been forced to walk when his dilapidated truck ran out of gas some miles down the road. Mother quickly prepared coffee, warmed up some leftover stew, and invited him to sit down to eat. After the stranger had eaten, Dad invited him to spend the night in the warm sauna, where a fire was kept going to prevent the water pipes from freezing.

The next morning, Dad gave the man enough gasoline to get him to the neighborhood store, and helped him to start the truck. (In those days, the anti-freeze solution was not as scientifically perfect as it is today, and engines were almost impossible to start in below-zero weather.)

For months afterward, we played a game called "Cold and Chilly Man." We never knew his name or anything about him. Some years later, he showed up at our door again. This time, he gave Mother a length of blue brocade fabric to repay her for the kindness she and Dad had shown him on that cold winter night.

OUR OWN ROOM

When I was eleven and Esther was thirteen, Dad decided to remodel the attic to create three bedrooms which were sadly needed. We girls were growing up, and had outgrown the sofa bed in the living room. Besides, after Elsie and Lauri had arrived, Mother and Dad's bedroom was over-flowing with their double bed, the baby's crib, and an old iron couch with drop-sides. I remember that couch very well. When the two sides were up, it provided a sleeping area as large as a double bed. With both sides down, it doubled as a sofa or settee. But when one side was up it was a dangerous place to sit; it would upset as soon as any weight was put on that side.

We anxiously watched the progress of the new rooms from the time Dad removed the old gabled dormer and built in a slanted-roof, three-window dormer where our new room would be. It was not a very large room, and the ceiling was low, but to us it represented a freedom and privacy we had never experienced before.

When the room was ready, Mother told us we could wallpaper it with some paper left over from her bedroom some years previously. So Esther and I, inexperienced as we were in the art of wallpapering, took on the project. We carefully measured, cut, and pasted, matching the pattern at each seam. All went well until we discovered, to our horror, there was not enough paper to do the final corner by the door. But that did not stop us; we simply pasted plain white ceiling paper in that corner. When the paste was dry, we got busy with our crayons and copied the blue-and-white floral pattern of the walls. Mother was so proud of our efforts, she talked about it for weeks, and was never too busy to show neighbors and friends the results of our handiwork. And, to be perfectly honest, we were quite proud of our work, too.

FASHIONS OF THE TIMES

Mother had her times of stubbornness. A classic example

involved the Red Cross. During the bleak times of the Depression, the Red Cross made a sincere effort to help the local farmers who were having a tough time making ends meet. Our family was no worse off than others in the area, but with seven children to feed and clothe it was a touch-and-go situation at times. When the Red Cross delivered a length of purple-and-white print material intended for school dresses for us, Mother wept. She wept, not because she was moved to tears by the generosity of the Red Cross, but because she felt that, somehow, she and Dad had failed us. Rather than have her girls show up in school with cotton print dresses of the same fabric as the other girls, she made curtains for the sauna from the Red Cross material and sewed dresses for us out of print feed sacks.

Mother's skill of creating something out of nothing kept us in decent clothing all through our growing-up years. She took old clothes which had been donated by our friends in Ely, and after ripping out all the seams, washing the pieces, and possibly dying them, she created "new" coats, skirts, and dresses for each of us. I still remember a coat which she created for me out of an old tan coat. She attempted to dye it a scarlet red, but the tan fabric did not take the dye too well, so the result was a brick color. She had a piece of fur, possibly squirrel or rabbit, to trim the collar. Everything went well until she started the final pressing.

The irons of the time, sad-irons, were aptly named and quite different from the irons we know today. The sad-iron was made of two parts: a wooden handle on a metal frame which clamped on to a heavy cast iron sole plate. Most families had at least two or three of the sole plates. The sole plates were heated on the woodburning stove until they were hot enough to smooth the wrinkles out of the items to be ironed. Occasionally, if the plates were heated two long, the results could be disastrous.

During the final pressing of my newly designed coat, Mother brought the sad-iron down on the fur-trimmed collar. Suddenly, there was a strong odor of burnt hair, and the fur puckered up. Mother had neglected to test the sad-iron with a wet finger; the damage looked hopeless to me, but not to Mother. She dampened the fur ever so slightly, and by gently pulling it in each direction, she managed to bring the collar almost back to its original shape. Later on, as I wore the coat, the fur developed cracks in all the weak places, and, gradually, the fur fell out. But by that time, I was wearing it for play, and the collar did not matter.

We girls were not the only ones benefiting from Mother's skill with needle, thread, and sewing machine. Paul, growing fast and, like many boys, hard on his clothes, was the recipient of a pair of woolen trousers, recycled from sleeves of a vintage World War I army coat. Whenever Paul wore the pants, he appeared to be somewhat bow-legged. Mother had neglected to remove the ease in the elbows of the sleeves. Fortunately, Paul was not of school age, he would have been the butt of many jokes!

Mother might have saved herself a lot of work and worry had she not been so set in her ways. With four, and later five, girls to dress and keep clean, many of her friends suggested that we would be better off in overalls. She resented such hints, and even though it might have meant less washing and ironing, she continued to dress us like little ladies.

Mother's attitudes never changed. When Esther and I were in eighth and ninth grades and became members of a local softball team, Mother once again refused to bend. The girls voted to wear denim jeans as the team uniform, but Mother went to Ely and bought us short-legged gym suits to wear for our ball games. So we sat on the benches, wearing our new green gym suits.

BROTHER PAUL

As Paul grew, so did his appetite. I well remember the summer when he had just turned three. Mother, Dad, Esther, Paul and I were making hay by an old railroad landing. This was wild hay, and was used primarily as bedding for the cow and her calf. Because it was several miles from home, Mother had packed a picnic lunch to take along. She had a quart jar of home-canned venison, bread and butter, pickled beets and, as a special treat, a half dozen hard-cooked eggs. We did not have chickens in those days, so eggs were a rather scarce item in the menu. Well, Paul consumed *three* of the eggs; Dad, Mother, and Esther each had one egg. That left me without an egg. To me, that was bad enough, but to hear Mother and Dad bragging about how baby Paul ate *three* eggs really hurt. For years they were to repeat the story about Paul's big appetite, but never once did anyone mention that I had been short-changed that day.

About this same time, Paul saw, for the first time, something that was to influence the rest of his life. This was the power line which provided electricity to the sleeping town of Babbitt. A few years prior to this, due to the taconite ore-mining operation, Babbitt had been a booming town. However, because of the cost of processing the ore, the plant closed in 1922, and the town became a Ghost Town. (Babbitt was to awaken from its deep sleep after World War II, when Reserve Mining took over the operation of the taconite industry.)

Nevertheless, when Paul first saw the power lines, he was totally fascinated by them and for the next few years, spent most of his time, and all of Mother's leftover carpet warp, building "power lines" wherever his fancy dictated. Eventually Mother had to exercise extreme caution whenever she stepped out of the barn with her milk pails; invariably, she became tangled in Paul's power lines, which he had erected while Mother was milking.

Paul's love affair and passion for power lines continued throughout his life. His education—in radio and electrical engineering—at Tri-State College provided the background for his life's work at Chance-Vought Air-Craft in Houston, Texas, and at Reserve Mining in Babbitt.

I can clearly remember details of Paul's early years. One detail in particular stands out in my mind. Paul had a morbid fear of having to try on new shoes. When the time came for him to go to Lamppa's or the Co-op store to be fitted for new shoes, the mere thought of having to try on shoes would make him cry and he would get sick to his stomach. Perhaps it was due to the fact that in his very tender years, Dad often brought home an assortment of shoes from a fire-sale. If the shoes fit we wore them; if they did not quite fit, we wore them anyway. Sometimes the shoes did not even match, but at least we weren't barefoot! Possibly Paul had memories of those ill-fitting shoes, and associated new shoes with foot pain.

As a young child, Paul had a way of usually getting what he wanted, and he also had a knack for getting us girls in trouble. Regardless of who was the rightful owner, if he wanted something, he got it. I once had a string of beads which I had salvaged from the ash pan of the kitchen range. Emptying the ashes from the stove was one of the chores I did every Saturday morning. Because Mother had a peculiar quirk of nature, assorted items would occasionally appear in the ashes. If we quarreled over a toy or possession, she snatched it and threw it in the stove. To her, this was probably a better, more permanent way of settling an argument than arbitration.

I had just brought the beads in, to show my prize, when Paul saw the beads and decided he wanted them. Martha, always ready to champion Paul, grabbed the beads from my hands, and in doing so brought her elbow crashing through the kitchen window. Dad, hearing the sound of breaking glass, came running into the kitchen. Not waiting for an explanation from anyone, not asking any questions as to what *did* happen, he merely grabbed me by the shoulder and took me into the sauna. In addition to its customary use, the sauna was often used as a place for punishment. I had never seen my father so angry. I knew it was futile to plead my case. By the time we reached the sauna, I had wet myself. Dad started to hit me with a long-handled sauna dipper, but Mother came in, just in time, with a birch bough. I got the whipping of my life, and for years I remembered that beating and the unfairness of it all. It was not until 1965, when Dad and I went to Finland, that he finally apologized to me. To my knowledge, Martha never had the opportunity to tell Dad the truth of the incident.

When Paul was little, he was often forced to wear our hand-me-down underwear. At times these had been patched and re-patched, as Mother squeezed every ounce of wear out of every article of clothing. Once, when Mother was buttoning Paul into an exceptionally patched pair of long underwear, Paul looked at Mother with a very sad expression and asked, *"Äiti, onko tämä pöly-raasu?"* (Mother, is this a dust rag?) This was but one of the occasions when Mother wished she could do more for her children.

When Paul was in the sixth grade in school, he entered the county-wide declamation contest at the local level. He competed in Oratory, and was fortunate to have as his coach a male teacher who had experience in that field. Paul won the local contest easily, went on to the district, and then to the county contest at Cook, where he won first place. When the winners presented their selections over the radio from a station in Duluth, we went to the neighbor's house to listen. Paul's oration was entitled, "I am an American." It depicted two Americans, one a descendant of the *Mayflower* settlers and the other a son of a Russian immigrant. This was before World War II—before the world was in a state of chaos.

One would think that because of Paul's early years, he would have grown up to be a real monster. Not so. Throughout the years, he became a real friend to his sisters, and we spent many happy hours together until World War II caused some major changes in our lives.

Shortly after the outbreak of World War II, Paul enlisted in the Navy. He served as a radio man. Before he was shipped to the Pacific Theater of Operations, he was stationed at San Pedro, California, and later at Houston, Texas. He was on the island of Okinawa at the time of the great Tidal Wave, and he sent many pictures back home to the farm showing the mass destruction caused by this natural disaster; a disaster which caused more devastation to the island than the Battle of Okinawa.

After his discharge from the Navy, Paul returned to the farm which he loved so well. However, he became restless with the uneventful farm life, and in 1950 took advantage of the G.I. Bill which made it possible for him, and thousands of other veterans, to go to college. He enrolled at Tri-State College in Angola, Indiana, where he received his degree in radio engineering in 1953.

Following his graduation from Tri-State, Paul accepted a good-paying job in Houston, Texas. It was not long, however, before his thoughts were back on the farm. So he packed his belongings and returned to his beloved Minnesota farm. After

Mother and Dad took their social security, they signed the farm over to Paul, with the understanding that they would have a home there as long as they lived. Paul raised beef cattle on the farm, and spent much of his time building and repairing fences and pastureland. He called the cows his "girls," and knew each one by name. After Mother passed away in September of 1965, Dad and Paul continued to live on the farm. Theirs was a unique relationship, with Dad doing the cooking and minor chores and Paul taking care of the bigger tasks. It was not long before Paul and Dad were doing the laundry together, too.

It was in May of 1980, after the passing of both Mother and Dad, when Paul died. It was one of the hardest days in our Kaurala family's history when the tragic news reached each member by phone. A terrible machinery accident had suddenly ended Paul's young life at the age of fifty-six. To think that Paul, who had always seemed invincible to us, would have his life snuffed out so tragically, was unbelievable and difficult for all of us to accept.

Some of us found consolation in the thought that this is what Paul would have wanted; to die on the farm, the place he was born and spent most of his life. It has been over fifteen years since that tragic day, but the years have not lessened the pain and emptiness, nor have the years dimmed the memory of our playmate, friend, and brother.

MARTHA

Being the first-born of seven children, Martha was very special in many ways. She was definitely the prettiest of the girls, with her abundance of dark hair, hazel eyes, and fair skin. Her personality was very outgoing, always upbeat, and forever seeking the positive side of life. She was generous to a fault, as was witnessed at a very tender age. Mother caught her pouring an entire container of rolled oats for the hundreds of sparrows in the yard. When Mother scolded her for this and Dad explained that the birds have a loving, Heavenly Father who will feed them, Martha indignantly replied, "He can't be much of a Heavenly Father if He makes them eat horse manure." The birds had been picking kernels of oats out of the horse manure in the backyard.

Another evidence of Martha's generosity surfaced when Mother was making a two-layer cake for her third birthday. The two layers were cooling on the table when Martha took one and presented it to Esther. When Mother tried to explain that the two layers were for her birthday cake, Martha said, matter-of-factly, "No birthday cake. Just give Esther a cake, too..."

Martha's life took a tragic turn when she was thirteen months old. Mother had given birth to Esther just two days previously. The attending mid-wife had used a disinfectant solution to clean the equipment in the lying-in room and for some unknown reason had placed the basin of strong disinfectant under the bed. With the speed and unpredictability of a tornado, Martha discovered the basin and downed the contents before she was found, unconscious, on the floor. She was rushed to the hospital and her stomach was pumped out. Even though she appeared to have suffered no serious damage from the near catastrophe, it is possible the trauma played a big part in her later life.

When Martha was ten years old, she began to have epileptic seizures. The first one occurred while she was spending a week visiting some friends in Ely. It just so happened that she had attended a movie the previous day, so Mother inferred that the movie was somehow responsible. Regardless of the cause of the seizures, Mother fell apart whenever one occurred. She assigned Ora and me as guardians of Martha. We were to see that she did not hurt herself when she fell. That summer passed without incident, and with medication the seizures appeared to be under control.

Martha continued her education through the sixth and seventh grades, gaining honors and recognition in many areas. In the sixth grade she had the lead as a school teacher—a role she loved—in the Christmas play. That same year, she won first prize at the State Fair for an original fire safety poster. In the Thanksgiving Day program, her soprano solo, "Swing the Shining Sickle," made me proud to be her sister. The following year she was named winner in a county-wide poetry contest.

Her eighth-grade year was going smoothly until one day in late winter, when she suffered a seizure in school. Sadly, she fell against the jacketed stove, and would have been severely burned had it not been for a classmate who pulled her away from the stove. As it was, she suffered burns about the neck and face. Because of the near-tragedy, and the resulting panic of the other students, it was decided for the peace of mind of the other students as well as for Martha's own safety, she would be better off in an institution.

The county nurse and the Board of Education took an active part in this decision. Before the end of the school year, Martha was sent to a colony for epileptics in Cambridge, Minnesota. The year was 1931, during the depths of the Great Depression. The county nurse came to the house and took Martha with her meager belongings to Virginia, Minnesota, where she spent a few days in a private home while the paperwork was completed for her admission to Cambridge. Even though I cannot pin-point the exact date, I do remember my little sister Elsie running up to the nurse and proudly showing-off her new long johns. This incident helped to lighten the mood somewhat; it brought a chuckle to everyone, and, for a moment at least, we forgot the seriousness of the day.

After the nurse's car left the driveway, we watched as it went down the snow-covered road, out of sight. No one spoke for some time until Dad said, "Let us not cry—be happy for Martha. She will be cured and come back to us soon." We did not realize this colony would be the first of many institutions Martha would experience over the final years of her short life.

When Martha first arrived at Cambridge, she wrote home frequently. She was enthusiastic about the many activities provided—Glee Club, church choir, drama, and crafts. During her first year there she sang and danced a solo number in the annual Fall Follies. Unfortunately, we were unable to attend this performance, but she wrote to us and described her act. The song was titled "There's a Tickling in My Toes."

When Martha was a resident at the Cambridge Colony for Epileptics, Mother made arrangements each summer to make the long trip to see her. Because our car was unfit for long distance driving, Mother had to beg a neighbor or friend for this trip. There were no four-lane highways in those days; even the highway to the Twin Cities was only a two-lane, largely unimproved road. A trip to Cambridge and back required two full days, with an overnight at a hotel. It was in 1933 when Mother, Esther, and I made the trip to see Martha. Mother packed a lunch in the old wicker picnic basket, and made a gallon of *Watkins Cherry Nectar* to take along. We stopped several times along the way to stretch our legs and to have a bite to eat. (Roadside rest stops and fast foods were as yet unheard of.) We visited Martha for several hours.

We spent the night in an old hotel building, which was certainly not one of the "Sir Walter Raleigh slept here" places. But it was the first time Esther and I had been in a hotel, so we looked upon it as a special treat. The next morning, before heading back, we visited with Martha again. We arrived at home quite late that night. Dad was glad to see us safe and sound. Even though Mother was depressed for several days after our visit, she eventually shook off her blues and began making plans for the next summer.

Our family was never the same after Martha left that snowy day. At the time, little was known or understood about the condition of epilepsy. In the sixty years since then, these colonies, as well as tuberculosis sanitariums and many mental institutions, have been eliminated. Had we known then what we know today—that epilepsy can be controlled by medication and proper therapy—this drastic action need not have been taken.

Martha was to spend the remainder of her short life in and out of institutions. During the summer of 1936 she was at home for eight weeks. This was a trying time for the entire family. Esther and I had summer jobs in Babbitt, so Ora, the next in line, was held responsible for Martha's care during the day. What was Mother thinking to put this huge responsibility on a fourteen-year-old child? But Mother would have no part of it. To her, the epilepsy was a form of curse, and no amount of argument would change Mother's mind.

When school reopened that fall, Martha was admitted to a state mental institution because the epileptic colony would not re-admit her after such a long absence. While in the mental institution, her health and mental state deteriorated rapidly. She passed away just before Christmas in 1939 at the age of twenty-two. The autopsy report showed she had tuberculosis of the stomach and intestines; it was this, not the epilepsy, which caused her death.

Shortly after Martha's death, all the family members had to undergo testing for tuberculosis. Esther and I were in Saint Paul at the time. I had to report to the University of Minnesota Health Service for the Mantoux skin test. There was a certain stigma attached to tuberculosis, and we were rather embarrassed at having to submit to the test. I have often thought about what would have happened to us if our tests had proved positive.

Over these many years, as I have thought about Martha, I have often wondered about what roads her life would have followed had she been able to remain with the family. Now as I sit alone with my memories of my childhood days, I miss her, shed silent tears, and hope she forgives us all for our stupidity and lack of compassion.

THE PIANO

In August of 1929, we were thrilled when a big, black truck drove into the yard. (All trucks were black in those days, as were most of the cars.) Two men came out of the truck, and after a few preliminaries, explained they had a brand-new piano on board and wanted to leave it for a few days, hoping we would decide to purchase it. Dad was not at home just then, and Mother's English was inadequate for the situation. So before we knew it, the piano was unloaded and wheeled into the living room. We girls kept our mouths shut, even though we knew the piano was a luxury we could ill afford. We had been taught never to interrupt grownups' conversations, so we maintained a golden silence throughout the episode.

That afternoon when Dad came home, he decided immediately that he wanted the piano and would somehow manage to pay for it. The arrangement was "ten dollars down and ten dollars a month" until the purchase price of two-hundred and ninety-five dollars was paid. He loved music, and regardless of the fact that he could not carry a tune in a milk pail, he was anxious to have his daughters learn to play a musical instrument.

After the bank failures in late 1929, it was difficult for Dad to meet the payments each month. However, by skimping a bit here and there, and cutting corners now and then, he somehow managed, and by the end of 1932 we were the sole owners of the piano.

Acquiring the piano was one thing, arranging music lessons was quite another. Even though Dad had petitioned the school board to assign a teacher with some musical background to our school, he had to borrow a teacher from a school five miles away. So, on Friday night, he picked up the teacher and brought her to our house for the weekend. Martha was a very apt pupil; she learned quickly, and in turn taught me the basic exercises, scales, and simple songs. After Martha was admitted to the Cambridge Colony for Epileptics, Mother did not allow anyone to touch the piano for months. In time she relented, and even arranged for me to take piano lessons. My musical education was somewhat haphazard; a few lessons here and a few lessons there. Nevertheless, I enjoyed it and even now, when I am going on eighty, I often play the organ, just to satisfy my thirst for live music.

MOTHER'S INFLUENCE

"Sugar rationing was in effect at the time,
but fortunately, Mother had purchased a
fifty-pound sack of sugar before
the rationing began..."

HOME ECONOMICS TRAINING

From the time we were toddlers, we were curious about what went on in Mother's kitchen. How she could take flour, milk, sugar, lard, and a few other ingredients, mix them together, and at one time produce bread, and the next time, sweet rolls, cake or cookies, was a mystery to us.

Mother took great pride in her culinary skills. She had worked as a domestic for several years prior to her marriage, and had learned to cook and bake hundreds of mouth-watering dishes. Most of her recipes were in her head; she never used a cookbook, but the results were always successful. She was never too busy to give each of us girls a little glob of dough which we rolled and shaped until it was almost black from our grubby hands. Thus, we learned the feel and texture of bread dough— how it differed from pie dough or cookie dough. As we grew older, we took turns kneading the huge batches of bread she made each week. Ten or twelve loaves were not unusual, with cardamom-flavored Finnish *Pulla* or coffee cake to provide the treat to go with the customary afternoon coffee. We learned, early in life, how to braid three or four ropes of dough to produce the fancy twists or braids of coffee cake.

When we were growing up, white bread was non-existent in

our home. Mother always baked wheat or rye bread, so whenever friends from Ely came to visit, they usually brought a loaf of sliced white bread from the bakery. We enjoyed that treat even more than we did the doughnuts, or "fry-cakes" as we called them, or the occasional Bismarks which they brought. These friends never came empty-handed, and when they left, Mother made sure they did not leave empty-handed. That is, all except for one lady who brought a bag full of stale, moldy doughnuts. We joked about the hard, moldy cakes for weeks.

Baking was not an easy matter with a woodburning range and a temperamental oven that would heat from 350 to 450 degrees Fahrenheit in a matter of minutes. Many were the times when an oven full of bread or cookies went from almost done to scorched in the wink of an eye. Brother Paul secretly prayed that the cookies, in particular, would suffer this fate. He was more than willing to eat the charred cookies and often consumed several dozen with a glass of milk.

Doughnuts were one of Mother's most special homemade treats. On her doughnut-making day she pushed a huge steamer-trunk into the doorway to keep us out of the kitchen. She did not want us underfoot for obvious reasons; cooking in hot grease over a woodburning fire was risky, to say the least. Besides, she needed to focus all her attention on the job at hand. When the doughnuts were ready we devoured them eagerly, with one regret: there were never quite enough to satisfy everyone's appetite. It would be a long time until the next doughnut-making day arrived.

Mother baked pies at least once every week. My favorite was raisin pie or blueberry pie. During the hot summer we picked quarts and quarts of wild blueberries which Mother canned for future use. When apples were plentiful in early fall, we had apple pie; but more often, I remember apple pie prepared from dried apples. I was never too fond of that, as there were very often sharp pieces or seeds in the dried apples. Mother scolded me when she caught me carefully picking these inedible bits out of my piece of pie. Rhubarb pie, while not one of my favorites, was quite often on the menu. Sometimes Mother mixed a few raisins into the rhubarb mixture to produce a different flavored pie.

Regardless of our personal likes and dislikes, to my knowledge there was never as much as a sliver of pie thrown out or wasted. When Mother passed away, one of Dad's first requests to me was for an apple pie. He peeled the apples, and together we made a pie, which, while not quite up to Mother's standards, nonetheless brought tears to his eyes as he said, "Just like Mother used to make."

Whenever I think back on those childhood days, I cannot help but marvel at Mother's ability to make desserts from such limited ingredients. Using lard, a little sugar, spices, flour, and liquid she produced cookies, cakes, and muffins unlike any I have eaten since. She had no ready-made mixes—in fact, she did not even have an electric mixer. Yet she made sponge cakes and jelly rolls that would make Betty Crocker sit up and take notice.

A chore we learned to tolerate, if not to enjoy, was churning butter. At least once a week, winter and summer, Mother set out the cream to become slightly sour. Then Esther and I, or Ora and I, took turns pushing the wooden dasher up and down in the five-gallon, tin-coated can. To make the chore go faster, and to relieve the monotony, we took turns chanting, "Come, butter, come." After an endless period of pumping and chanting, the dasher suddenly became heavy, and we heard the unmistakable sound of butter thumping in the churn. After a few more pumps, the butter had gathered enough to be easily separated from the buttermilk. Then the butter was lifted out with the wooden butter spoon Dad had carved years ago.

The real buttermilk was poured into pitchers, to be kept in a cool place where it slowly soured to become what the Finns called *Pitkä piimä* or "long buttermilk," so-called because it literally stretched when it was poured. The new butter was washed in several changes of cold water and worked until every trace of milk was removed. Then it was salted to taste, usually to Mother's taste as she did not trust us with this part of butter-making, after which it was packed into a three-pound crock and covered with parchment paper. Oh, happy were the days before cholesterol was a problem!

THE WAR YEARS

When the Japanese attacked Pearl Harbor on December 7, 1941, most of the able-bodied young men in our area were drafted into military service. They were neighbors and friends, classmates, brothers of classmates, boyfriends, and some were newly married husbands.

Mother and Father were deeply touched as they read the news and learned the names of the inductees. The list grew longer each week. Mother wanted to do something for the boys at Christmas. At her Victory Club meeting, she suggested the group make cookies to send the servicemen. When she was voted down, she came home with a firm resolution to undertake the project herself.

Having graduated from the University of Minnesota in July, I was at home at the time. So Mother and I baked cookies for days and packed boxes to send to the servicemen. Even though the cookies were not ready in time for Christmas, we mailed twenty-five to thirty boxes so each soldier from our area received a box by the middle of January. Sugar rationing was in effect at the time, but fortunately Mother had purchased a fifty-pound sack of sugar before the rationing began, so we were able to make the dozens and dozens of cookies.

When the thank-you notes started coming in, Mother treasured each one. By the end of March, she had a shoe box full of notes from grateful servicemen. She kept these notes until her death. In the winter of 1991, during Operation Desert Storm, I remembered Mother and her one-woman Operation Cheer.

In 1937, when Esther decided to enroll at Ely Junior College, I enrolled in Virginia Junior college. For the next two years, while we attended college, we did not see much of each other. In 1939, when I went to the University of Minnesota to complete my college work, our lives converged again for two more years. We were well-known on the Farm Campus (as the St. Paul campus was called). Esther was known by the nick-name "Fox" and I was "Buzz," a nick-name which has stuck with me all these years. Esther's nick-name came about when she was quite small. Martha took to calling

85

her "Ette," then "Ettu-Kettu." Since Kettu is Finnish for a fox, "Fox" made sense.

During my two years at the University, Esther continued to work at Montgomery Ward's huge mail order house. Then, shortly before America's involvement in World War II, she went to work at International Harvester, which was producing materials for the defense industries to prepare America for the inevitable war.

During the war years, our lives, like the lives of many other families, went in different directions. I was a member of the Women's Army Corps., stationed in California. The only contact my sister and I had was during my brief furloughs. It was not until the summer of 1949 when the family was finally together again.

MOTHER'S TREASURES

From the time we were old enough to understand, certain things were forbidden. Most definitely, one of these was the top drawer of the tall bookcase secretary with the bulging glass front. We were free to explore the contents of the second drawer which held an accumulation of Christmas cards from years past, and the third drawer, where there was an assortment of old photographs. But the top drawer was Mother's private domain, and it was always kept locked. Even though the key was usually available, we never dreamed of using it to investigate the mysteries the drawer held. For years, we imagined Mother had a secret bank account or, at least, a hidden cash box in it.

When Mother passed away, Dad ceremoniously handed the key to Esther, saying, "Now, the girls can dig in Mother's secret drawer." Imagine our reactions when we opened the drawer and discovered, not money or bank books, but a collection of what was, to Mother, more precious than money. There were brittle, faded Mother's Day cards which we had made on manila paper, a special Mother's Day resolution painstakingly printed by Paul when he was in second grade, yellowed newspaper clippings of Honor Roll listings when we were at Ely High School, and the sterling silver pin Paul was awarded when he won first place in the county declamation contest. There were copies of mimeographed newsletters of World War II servicemen and, in a shoe box tied with a blue ribbon, were the thank-you letters Mother received from the servicemen acknowledging the cookies she sent shortly after the attack on Pearl Harbor.

Those were Mother's treasures, kept safely locked all those years in the top drawer of the secretary. Little did we dream that these were so precious to her. They were treasures that were hers alone. Treasures no amount of money could buy. They represented the tributes that were hers just by virtue of being our mother. Sometimes we were saddened by the fact that Mother was seldom one to openly demonstrate her love for us, yet we knew she loved each of us in her own special way.

SEX EDUCATION

We learned many of the facts of life by observing the animals on the farm. In those days, when dogs were dogs and were neither spayed or neutered, cats were free to roam, and barnyard roosters pursued hens all day long, sex education was not obtained through classroom study and homework. When our dog, Rags, entertained the neighbor's dog, Rascal, overnight, and when the cat, Eva, disappeared for several days, we knew that before too long there would be new puppies or kittens or both.

And so there were. Rags often gave birth to her pups in the coldest part of the winter. Dad usually hunted them out and eliminated all but one so Rags could enjoy the responsibilities of Motherhood for a few weeks. Before the puppy was too firmly entrenched in our affections, Dad found it a home with one of the neighbors.

Sex education was not limited to cats and dogs; during our growing-up years we learned how a mother hen sits on her nest of eggs for several weeks before the chicks hatch. We knew the rooster's attack on the hen had something to do with whether the eggs hatched or became rotten. This was very obvious one summer when we had a flock of hens but no rooster. We found several nests of rotten eggs, where would-be mother hens had tried to hatch them. One summer, a friend of ours presented us with some rabbits. They were kept in the old *Savu-Sauna* (Smoke-Bath House, so-called because it had no chimney to let out the smoke.) Whenever we had time on our hands, we went to play with the rabbits. Usually, the male rabbit was busy with a female bunny and did not wish to be bothered. The two other female rabbits were more willing to be friendly. In a few weeks, the rabbit population trebled. That was when Mother decided it was time for some rabbit stew. Mother remarked that it was a good thing people did not multiply at the same rate rabbits did.

Our mother never sat down with us to explain the facts of life. I suppose she felt we would learn these things in due time; after all, she never had sex education classes in Finland when she was a girl. I learned from the older girls in school—one of the advantages of the outdoor toilet. Hearing the older girls talk about "the curse," "monthly bleeds," pregnancy, and the "change of life" stirred my imagination. I thought the change of life meant a mysterious transition into another form of life. I wondered how I would know when the change was imminent, and what form of life I would change into.

Shortly before my fourteenth birthday, I awoke one morning to find I had become a woman overnight. Because Mother had never told me too many details about this event, I chose to keep it to myself. My sister, Esther, was a year and a half older and had not yet had this experience, so I was ashamed it had happened to me. I scrounged around in Mother's rag box and found a clean, white sack which had been filled with salt at one time. After some more searching, I found some pieces of underwear, which I stuffed into the salt sack to make a sanitary napkin, and I proceeded to pin it to my underwear. In those days, we did not have money for commercial feminine hygiene products, we had to use what was available and be willing to wash the rags out for reuse. I kept the secret for several months, until one day Mother asked me point-blank, and I admitted having been a woman for some time.

Another recollection from my adolescence was perspiration

and the resulting odor. How I hated myself at times when I perspired and the odor wafted around me. I wished we had money for deodorants or antiperspirants. When Lux soap carried ads in magazines promoting its deodorant qualities, I took a piece of soap and rubbed it into my armpits, hoping it would destroy the smell. Later, when money was not as scarce, I remember buying my first bottle of *ODO-RO-NO* which kept me dry and odor-free. It also rotted-out the armpits of my clothes.

As I grew older, these bits of information began to fall into place. By the time I was ready for high school I knew enough about cows and bulls to know that a bull was no longer needed for a cow to become pregnant. We no longer had to drive a cow to the neighbor's bull; artificial insemination had changed all of that.

MOTHER THE RECYCLER

In the 1920s and 1930s, recycling was not an option, it was a way of life. Mother recycled everything for, as she put it, everything had more than one use. The feed and flour sacks which accumulated each week were used for many household items. The burlap bags from cattle feed were used for bagging potatoes during digging time. Later on they were cut to make smaller bags when Dad sold produce in Ely. When the burlap was too far gone to be used for anything else, it made a soft bed for Rags or one of the other dogs.

I was probably five years old when Mother made me a beautiful woolen dress. It was recycled from a skirt donated to us by one of Mother's friends in Ely. The fabric was predominantly green with a light tan stripe running down its length. Its main features were a Peter Pan collar and long, cuffed sleeves. The one feature which set this dress apart from all other dresses was the row of green glass buttons which went from the neck-line to the hem. As if green glass was not enough, these buttons also had a rim of gold around the edge, and were shaped almost like a cup. When the light shone on the buttons, they reflected it in all directions. I often sat in the sunlight just so I could watch the magic prisms dancing on my dress.

One Sunday afternoon, Mother took Martha and Esther for a visit to the neighbor's. I cried because Mother would not let me go with them. It was a cold day, and she thought I would be better off at home with Dad, Ora, and Paul.

After Mother and the older girls left, I cried for a while. Then I resolved to get even with Mother. As I dried my tears and wiped my nose, I knew what I was going to do. I knew the scissors were in the top drawer of the sewing machine cabinet. So, I sneaked past Dad, who was the baby-sitter, and, hiding the scissors behind me, slipped upstairs to where the dress was hanging. Without any other thought except revenge, I proceeded to cut all of the buttons off the dress. I cut not only the buttons, but a circle of cloth under each button. The deed done, I carefully slipped downstairs and replaced the scissors in their customary place.

Mother did not discover my misdeed for several days. I was beginning to think it had all been in vain, but she found the dress when she went upstairs to put some clothes away. Needless to say, she was very angry with me. But I did not get the spanking I expected. She took her anger out on Dad, who had been, after all, the baby-sitter, and should have kept a closer eye on his charges.

Was the dress beyond repair? Not by a long shot! Mother, fortunately, had a few scraps of fabric left, so she made a new button hole strip for the dress. The glass buttons, however, could not be replaced nor found. Mother found some dark brown shoe-button type buttons for the dress. Every time I wore the dress, I felt pangs of guilt for what I had done. Literally, I had bitten off my own nose to spite my own face.

To her dying day, Mother never found the buttons. For the first few days, she thought perhaps I had swallowed them. The only logical conclusion she reached was I had dropped them between the two-by-fours in the unfinished attic. Now, almost 70 years later, I do not remember what I did with those glass buttons.

Mother let nothing go to waste. When a flour sack was emptied, Mother ripped out the seams and slightly dampened the material. Then she rubbed a bar of *Fels Naptha Soap* over the lettering, rolled up the damp fabric and left it overnight. The next day, she washed it out. The result was a square of soft, white material. Four of them sewed together with flat felled seams made a bed sheet. One sack, joined along two sides, and hemmed at the end, made a pillow case. Another sack, hemmed on all four sides, made a generous dish-towel. The smaller sacks, such as from sugar, made bloomers and vests, and the smallest of all, salt sacks, were made into handkerchiefs.

In the winter months, when Mother had to remain indoors~ she worked at her spinning. We were called upon to help as she recycled old woolen sweaters, socks, and mittens to make re-worked wool. She cut the old garments into narrow strips, about an inch wide, and our job was to pull these apart into ravelings. Then she used her wool cards from Finland to comb the ravelings with some new wool to make fluffy lengths which were then spun into yarn.

Sometimes, instead of making the fluffy lengths for spinning, she made soft rectangles of the wool; these were the size of the cards. After she had several boxes full of woolen rectangles, she laid them out on an old sheet, layering them to make a soft woolen batt for a quilt. After this, she laid another old sheet or worn blanket over the multi-layered wool and began to stitch through it to complete the batt. Finally, the edges were whip-stitched all around, or if Mother was especially ambitious, a binding was applied to the edges. This was necessary so the batt could be handled without falling apart.

Next, the quilt top and lining were sewn together along three sides, leaving one end open for the final assembling of the quilt. Putting the batt inside the quilt required Mother and us girls to work as a team. With the quilt-cover-and-lining laid wrong side out on the floor, Mother carefully laid the prepared batt over it. Then, with Mother in the center and a girl at each end, we attacked the job of rolling the batt into the cover. We had to be careful to keep rolling evenly so the batt would not bunch up inside the cover. When we reached the other end, voila! The batt was inside, and the quilt was ready to be tacked.

Here, again, we worked as a team. Mother made the first row

of tacks, or knots, with woolen yarn. Using her knots as a guide, we made row after row of knots to fasten the batt to the cover. The final step, completing the quilt, was closing the end. Mother usually did this by hand with heavy thread, whip-stitching the raw ends together.

I still have a quilt which she made for me forty-five years ago, and each night, as I wrap myself up in the warm, wool-filled comforter, I think of Mother and her labors of love. It is almost like having her arms around me once more.

Mother's resourcefulness was evident in other areas as well. When the hog was slaughtered around Thanksgiving time each fall, Mother recycled every part of it except the squeal. Dad often joked that Mother would have been the one to find a use for it, had it been possible. She used the head, feet, and the bony parts to make the most delicious head cheese. Here again, we girls had to pick the bits of meat off the bones after Mother had roasted them for hours in the big, blue enamelware roaster. It was a tedious job, but the end product was worth it.

From the pork liver she made *Maksa Kakkuja*, which were liver dumplings. These were Brother Paul's favorite treat. For them, Mother ground partially frozen liver (it was easier to handle in a semi-frozen state). Then she mixed it with egg, flour, and seasonings to produce a dough which she shaped into patties. These were dropped into boiling water and simmered until they floated to the top. They were served with melted butter and fried onions. . . Delicious!

When a new calf was born, Mother milked the beestings (the first milk from the mother cow) and used it to make a tasty quick cake called *Kropsu*. It was quite chewy, but with gobs of butter and jam or jelly it was delicious.

Mother's main hobby (if, indeed, it could be considered as such) was weaving rag rugs. Whenever a garment had passed the stage of being wearable or repairable, it was washed and dried and, usually, ironed. Then it was thrown into the box in the stairwell pantry. When Mother had nothing else to do, she took out her scissors and cut the garment into strips which were rolled into balls for her weaving.

Dad made Mother's rug loom years ago, after Mother and a neighbor lady got into a dispute over the use of the traveling loom. Ever since I can remember, Mother sat at her loom—first it was in the old shed by the garage, then it was moved to the hay-mow part of the barn where she continued to weave her rugs on a regular basis until shortly before her death.

Mother purchased her warp-yarn from Sears or Ward's, usually buying enough to provide twenty-five or thirty yards of warp. Whenever there was a wedding, anniversary, housewarming, or any occasion calling for a gift, Mother's contribution was a well-made rug. She often joked that, if laid end-to-end, her rugs would go around the world at the equator.

Mother believed that everything in life was recyclable, from the cow manure in the fields to the coffee grounds she put in her flower beds. Yes, Mother was truly a recycler—long before the need to recycle was established.

EVENTS OF THE TIMES

"In the 1930s, most of our neighbors had radios.
We were often invited to one of the neighbor's
homes to listen to a special broadcast."

HEADLINE NEWS

In the spring of 1927, the front-page news centered around the kidnap-for-ransom and brutal murder of a twelve-year-old girl in California. The girl's name was Marian Parker, and even though there were hundreds of miles between us and California, the story touched us deeply. For weeks after her mutilated body was discovered we were terrified that her murderer, Edward Hickman, would somehow manage to come to our area and kill one of us. We were afraid to go out alone~ not even to the outhouse, until we were sure Hickman had been apprehended. When the news came that Mr. Hickman had been hanged for his crime, we finally let go of our fears.

Another news story which caused us much concern was the kidnapping of the Lindbergh baby in March of 1933. We shared with the rest of America in the sorrow of this tragedy. Having seen pictures of the beautiful, curly-haired toddler, we wondered how anyone could be so heartless as to snatch him from his crib, and then to murder him for money. For once, we were glad to be poor; at least, we were reasonably sure no one would want to kidnap us for ransom.

The years between 1931 and 1934 were famous for other names, among them, Bonnie and Clyde, "Baby-Face" Nelson,

"Bugs" Moran, and John Dillinger. These were the years of the big gangsters and as the stories circulated, we worried that they would appear in our area. Actually, John Dillinger escaped from the police in Saint Paul, Minnesota, so it was not totally improbable to expect him to show up in our community which was barely 200 miles away. In time, most of these men and women were killed or captured by police. Al Capone was sent to jail. Thus ended our restless days and sleepless nights.

THE RADIO

In the 1930s, most of our neighbors had radios. We were often invited to one of the neighbor's homes to listen to a special broadcast. I remember, in particular, the time in 1934 when the whole family went to the Olson's to listen to the Max Baer-Prime Carnera championship fight. Paul, not quite eleven at the time, was totally absorbed in the broadcast, and for weeks afterward he imitated the announcer's manner and delivery.

Then there was the Christmas when we were invited to the Mattson's home for Christmas dinner. All day long we listened to Christmas music on their radio, and, for the first time, Mother admitted she enjoyed it. Until then she and Dad had been adamantly opposed to what they called "canned music."

It was not until the fall of 1936 that we owned our first radio. Dad bought it in Ely, and when he brought it home, we felt that the Kauralas had finally arrived. Every morning we listened to the news, followed by a request program where listeners could mail in their request for a certain song, for a special occasion.

On the morning of October 8th, we had a good reason for listening. It was Mother's birthday, and we had secretly sent in a request for a song to be played in her honor. We had quite a time convincing Mother to put off her milking chores for a few minutes while we listened to the program. When her name was announced, and the D. J. played the song "Silver Threads Among the Gold," Mother cried. Her tears were contagious. Before the song was over, we were all in tears. To Mother, this was truly a birthday to remember.

The radio provided us with many hours of pleasure; listening to the *Lucky Strike Hit Parade, Amos and Andy, Fibber McGee and Mollie,* and in later years, Brother Paul's favorite program, *The Lone Ranger.* In the mid-fifties television came to the area, and the radio was no longer the prime source of entertainment.

POLITICS AND ORGANIZATIONS

Mother and Dad, while seeing eye-to-eye on many things, nevertheless held opposite views when it came to politics. Mother claimed to be a Democrat through and through, while Dad voted for the candidate, not the party. Mother used to tell Dad it was useless for him to vote, as he was merely cancelling her vote. However, there were two candidates they did agree on, Franklin D. Roosevelt and John F. Kennedy. When President Kennedy was assassinated, both Mother and Dad grieved as though he had been their own. No matter the outcome of an election, they accepted the result as the voice of the people, and as United States citizens, they were proud to have a voice in the government.

Before her marriage, Mother belonged to several organizations, among them, the Daughters of Kalevala, the Finnish Temperance Society, and the church choir. She was forced to give up these groups after they moved to the country, but she continued to keep a small flame of interest flickering, particularly in the area of church music. She spent hours teaching us to sing Finnish songs. We learned the Finnish words to "Silent Night" and other Christmas songs, and when Dad came home from his work in the mines in Ely, we would line up near the door and sing, *"Enkeli taivaan lausui näin"* or *"Joulu Yö, Juhla Yö."*

I was about nine years old when Mother entertained the ladies' church group at our house. Because she wanted everything to be just perfect, she borrowed a matching set of six cups and saucers. These were made of real porcelain, not like the heavy earthenware cups and saucers we used everyday.

After the last guest had left, and Mother had carefully washed and dried the chinaware, she breathed a sigh of relief to think they were still intact. About that time, I came rushing into the kitchen and accidentally brushed up against the counter and caused not just one, but all six cups and saucers to go crashing to the hardwood floor. I was panic stricken, to say the least, and a few minutes later, I felt the birch bough on my backside. Mother scolded me for being so careless, but she blamed herself for leaving the dishes in such a vulnerable place. The next day, Dad took Mother to Ely, where she hunted in vain for identical cups and saucers. She bought some that, while not identical to the ones she had borrowed, were close enough, and so her neighbor accepted them, with Mother's apology. Mother never borrowed dishes after that.

Every year, Mother planned a Christmas program. Usually it involved only us, but often the neighbor's children were included, too. Mother loved to act as the director of the production, and she spent many hours rehearsing us for the program. One year, she directed a whole group of neighborhood children in a Mother's Day program which was held at School #74. The program involved not only songs and recitations, but a rather long play as well—in Finnish! Yes, the Daughters of Kalevala and the Temperance Society lost a valuable member when Mother moved to the country.

While I am on the subject of Mother's club activities, I am reminded of a pair of Mother's black boots which had high tops and pointed toes. We called them her "meeting shoes," because she used to wear them to her meetings when we still lived in Ely. After the move to the farm, the boots gathered dust on the floor of the upstairs until one day Martha got the bright idea to chop off the pointed toes; the result was the first pair of open-toed shoes.

During World War II, both Mother and Dad were very active in defense activities and in the Finnish Relief Program. Even though Finland was, technically, on the wrong side of the fence, many of the American Finns were first and second-generation Finns, and were deeply concerned over the problems facing their relatives and friends in Finland. Every week or two, Mother sent a box of food or clothing to either her or Dad's relatives. Years later, when I went to Finland with Dad, it was gratifying to hear how

Mother's packages had helped our cousins. Several of them said had it not been for those boxes from America, they would never have made it through the war and the difficult times which followed when the country was trying to recover from its wounds.

LEAVING THE FARM

In the fall of 1939, I had finished my first two years of Home Economics studies at Virginia Junior College, and was now ready to go to the Twin Cities to complete my education and get a degree in Dietetics.

Mother and Dad were planning to send me to Saint Paul by myself; the mere thought of this caused nightmares of the worst kind. When the day of my departure arrived, I pleaded with Mother to let Esther go with me. After considerable hemming and hawing, it was decided, we would go together. We had to have train fare and a little extra cash. By the time the fare was paid, there was exactly four dollars and fifty cents for our mad money. The D.M. & I.R. train left Embarrass that afternoon, and after a five-hour wait in Duluth, we boarded the Great Northern train to Saint Paul. We rode all night, arriving in Saint Paul around 6:00 A.M.

The Union Depot in Saint Paul was a huge place teeming with people. Mother and Dad had cautioned us not to speak to anyone except those wearing official uniforms. We sat on the hard wooden benches for several hours before we finally gathered enough courage to approach a lady seated at the booth labeled "Traveler's Aid." If ever there were travelers who needed aid, it was Esther and me. We were as desperate as they came. The Traveler's Aid was an elderly woman who took us under her wing, and helped us in many ways. She directed us to the street car stop, wrote down the names and numbers of the cars we had to ride to get to the Saint Paul campus of the University, and she even allowed us to leave our luggage (such as it was) at her station so we would not have to spend our limited cash to pay for a locker.

Well, we made it to the Saint Paul campus, and I went through the routine of class registration while Esther pored over the help wanted ads on the bulletin board of the Administration Building. Then, we decided to separate. I went to attend a tea for freshmen and transfer students, and Esther went for an interview in response to one of the ads. Unfortunately, we did not make any arrangements to meet at any specific time or place.

When the tea was over, I decided to go back to the Union Station, worried that our friend in the Traveler's Aid booth might have gone off duty. After all, she was guarding our luggage, which included not only our meager wardrobes, but also our box of goodies which Mother had packed. In it was a loaf of homemade bread, a small jar of home-churned butter, a box of *Krispy Crackers,* some homemade cookies, and a few apples.

I managed to make the first transfer point on the route, but missed the second, and got off the street car somewhere near the State Capitol Building. For a minute I was panic-stricken, but I resolved to make it to the Union Station on foot. I had no money to buy another token, and there was no choice but to walk. How I ever managed to reach my destination, I will never know—St. Christopher must have been directing my footsteps.

About two hours later, Esther came limping into the station. Relieved as I was to see her, I was amazed to learn she, too, had gotten off the street car at the same corner as I had. She had on a new pair of loafers, and, because they were not broken-in, she had developed a huge blister on her heel. The blister ruptured before she reached the station, and the resulting infection took several weeks to heal.

Our friend at the Traveler's Aid booth felt sorry for us and took us to her home for the night. She had a lovely apartment not far from the station. There was a Murphy Bed hidden in the wall. We had never heard of a bed in the wall, but it was a haven for us, and we slept soundly after having spent the previous night on the train.

The next morning, we gathered up our belongings and went back to the campus. The Traveler's Aid lady had a nephew who drove us around because Esther was unable to walk very far with her sore foot. We found a room for rent in a home near campus, and we moved in. The bed was not the most comfortable in the world, but it was a clean place, and we appreciated its close proximity to the campus.

That afternoon, Esther found employment in the home of a professor. She worked there for a few weeks until she was called to work in the billing department at Montgomery Ward's. Then, I took over her job, working at the professor's home after school three evenings a week. I was paid twenty-five cents an hour, plus supper. We were on our way!

After we were settled in, I in my classes and Esther in her job, things were a bit easier. I was approved for student aid under President Roosevelt's National Youth Administration. I was allowed to earn the magnificent sum of twenty-five dollars a month, at the rate of twenty-five cents per hour. I was assigned to work under one of the instructors in the Home Economics department. Esther helped me whenever I had a cash flow problem. Lunch at the cafeteria cost fifteen cents, and the evening meal was twenty-five cents, without dessert. (With dessert, it was thirty cents.)

Toward the end of the month, before the N.Y.A. check came through, I had to depend on Esther for my lunch money. One morning I was unusually rushed and left for my classes without the fifteen cents Esther had laid out for me. My first class was at the Minneapolis Campus. By the time I got back to the Saint Paul Campus, my stomach was making hungry noises, and I was wondering how I would survive the rest of the day without food.

I walked into the Student Union Building, and there, on the window sill, was a brown paper bag. No one else was around, so I went to take a closer look at the bag. Inside was a lovely lunch— a bologna sandwich, some oatmeal cookies, and an apple. Despite a few pangs of guilt, I helped myself to the lunch. When I went home that night, I wrote to Mother, telling her how God had provided lunch for me when I was in such dire need. Three days later, Mother wrote back, giving me a lecture, reminding me of the Ten Commandments, the eighth of which specifically states: "Thou Shalt Not Steal." Along with the lecture was a rather soiled, time-worn five-dollar bill.

There would be other times my funds would run low, and I

would look Hunger in the eyes, but I was never again tempted to take anything that did not belong to me. Mother's lecture stayed with me and saw me through many difficult times.

I graduated from the University in July of 1941. I have often marvelled how Esther and I survived those first few days. Mother and Dad must have had great faith in us and in our ability to cope with difficulty. But then, we were endowed with Finnish *Sisu*, which is what Mother and Dad had to have to leave their homes in Finland, and face the untold challenges life in a new country. Our life on the farm had given us the richness of understanding, the caring support and the skills we needed to know we could make it— even on our own.

Closing Thoughts

As I look back on my childhood years, I remember not only the hardships and sacrifices we endured, but also the satisfaction of making it as a family. Wearing hand-me-down shoes and clothes helped reinforce Mother's and Dad's teaching that appearances are not the most important things in life. What was inside the person was what counted; superficial wrappings could easily be stripped away, but the inner soul represented the real person.

Our pride in our Finnish heritage was nurtured from the time we were old enough to understand that we were the first generation of Finnish Americans from Mother's and Dad's families. Never was I more aware of this pride than when I visited Finland in 1966. I received a warm welcome wherever I went because I spoke the language and thus proved to the Finnish Finns that some of the American Finns cared enough about their heritage to learn to speak, read, and write the language.

Even though my years on the farm represent less than a quarter of my life, I will always feel that my roots are there. I have spent the last forty-eight years in Pennsylvania, but I will always think of the farm in northern Minnesota as my real home.

Printed in the United States
144901LV00002B/2/P